AF254863

READINGWARRIOR

Tongan Heroes
by David Riley

Published by Reading Warrior
Auckland, New Zealand

First edition 2016

ISBN 978-0-473-35244-8

Designed and typeset by Bronwen Billinghurst (i-set-type)

TONGAN HEROES

Written by David Riley
Illustrated by Michel Mulipola

This book is dedicated to Tongan young people

"Tō ē to'a kae tu'u ē to'a."

One warrior stricken, another warrior arisen.

'Oku 'uhinga ki ha mole ha taha mahu'inga kae toe fetongi mai 'e ha taha tatau,

'o hangē ko e mate ha to'a kae toe fetongi mai 'e ha to'a.

When a notable person dies, they are replaced by someone of the same calibre.

"Lusia ki taulanga."

Though weather-worn, the boat sails right into the harbour.

'Oku 'uhinga ki ha taha kuo fepaki mo ha ngaahi faingata'a kae tutui pē

ke a'u ki he feitu'u 'oku taumu'a ki ai

When someone faces many obstacles,

but is determined to press on to their destination.

Reed Book of Tongan Proverbs

'Okusitino Māhina

CONTENTS

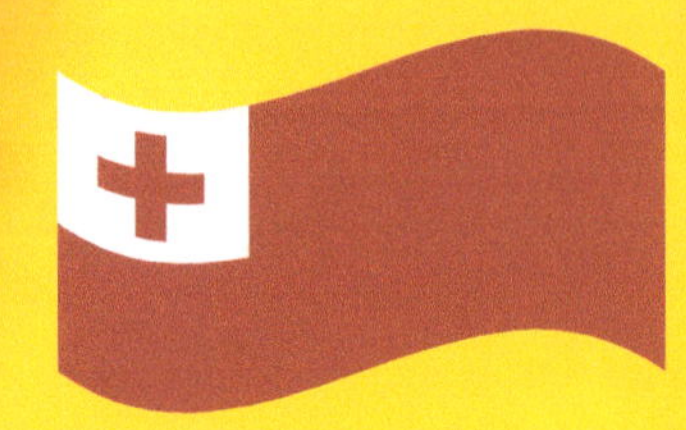

FOREWORD

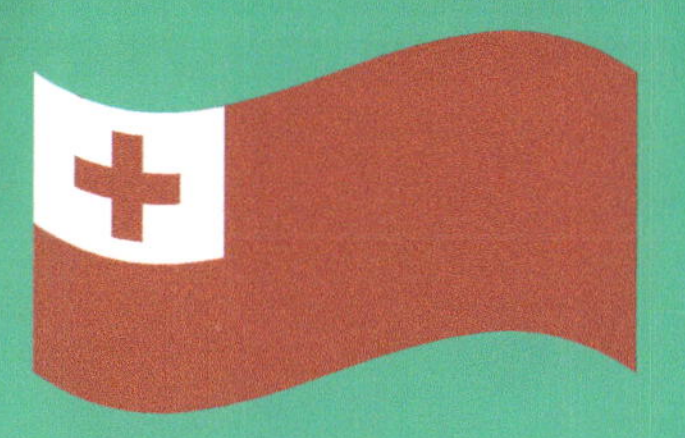

Ko e kuonga mo hono tangata is a Tongan saying which means that every era has its heroes and heroines.

This exciting book, written by high school teacher David Riley, tells the inspirational stories of such people - of Tongans who were and are outstanding in their time and field and as people.

A hero or heroine is, as we say in Tongan, *hangē ha fanā fotū*, like a mast showing above the horizon.

It's a metaphor for someone who stands out as a conspicuous example of achievement or honour.

These stories are not only inspiring, they are also informative and illuminating. Like our fananga, our traditional Tongan folktales, they carry important messages, particularly for our young people, of encouragement and hope; and of pride in our heritage and Tongan-ness.

They contribute to the celebration of our identity as a people both in Tonga and around the world.

I congratulate David for putting these stories together in one volume, a cross-section of outstanding Tongans across time and space.

The book will be a valuable resource that provides readers with a convenient and enjoyable way to learn about Tongan people, while at the same time recording something of our traditions and history.

Mālō ʻaupito David, and I look forward to a time when these stories can be read in Tongan also.

Happy reading!

ʻOfa atu,

Melenaite Taumoefolau, PhD
Centre for Pacific Studies
University of Auckland

Nuku'alofa
TONGA
Tongatapu
Eua
N
Vava'u
Ha'apai
Niuas
Note: Islands not drawn to scale

INTRODUCTION

Tongan Heroes is the third book in a series called Pasifika Heroes. *We Are the Rock* (Niuean heroes) was the first book in the series and was followed by *Samoan Heroes*.

A hero in these books is defined as a person who did something remarkable that helped or inspires others in some way.

Some heroes are famous in their own village, community or family.

Other heroes are known by lots of people, like many of the people in this book.

The Tongan Islands might be small in terms of landmass, but the achievers who come from these islands don't think small. They are people who have made a huge impact on our world.

In this book you'll read about a selection of contemporary, historical and legendary Tongan achievers who:

- accomplished things no one before them had

- reached world-class level in their chosen fields

- acted in inspirational ways

The people in this book faced the same challenges we all do.

They are not perfect and sometimes they made mistakes - but they persevered to make their dreams come true.

Very few of them could have achieved success without their faith and the support of family and friends.

In other words, they're people just like me and you!

A note about the use of oral histories

The legends and historical accounts in this book are not necessarily factual. It is the nature of oral history and traditions that alternative versions of these stories also exist.

THE FIRST TONGANS

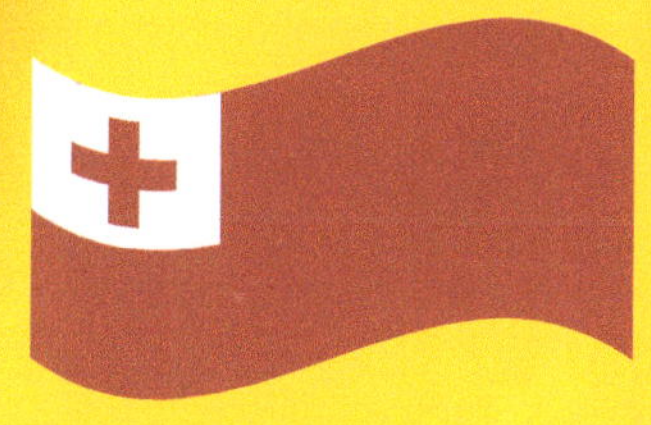

Taufulifonua had three sons: Hikule'o, Maui and Tangaloa. Hikule'o was in charge of Pulotu (a paradise north of Tonga), Maui looked after Lalotonga (the underworld) and Tangaloa ruled the sky.

Tangaloa had four sons: Tangaloa Tamapo'uli 'Alamafoa, Tangaloa 'Eitumatupu'a, Tangaloa 'Atulongolongo and Tangaloa Tufunga.

From his home in the sky, Tangaloa often gazed at the huge blue ocean below. "There could be so much more to you," he thought.

Tangaloa's youngest son - Tufunga - was a carver. Tangaloa told him to drop some wood chips into the ocean. As Tufunga did this the chips formed into an island, known today as 'Eua.

He threw more chips down and they became the islands Kao and Tofua.

"Those islands are beautiful," Tangaloa said. "But I believe there's a lot more potential in that ocean."

Tangaloa told 'Atulongolongo to see if he could find any more land. 'Atulongolongo changed into the form of a dove and flew down. He didn't find any land, but he did find a reef lying just below the surface of the water.

'Atulongolongo watched the reef gradually rise and become an island (known today as 'Ata).

One day, 'Atulongolongo dropped a seed from his beak and the seed grew into a fue vine that spread across the whole island.

'Atulongolongo pecked at the root of the vine. The root became rotten and a worm grew inside it. 'Atulongolongo pecked at the worm and it split into two parts.

The top piece changed into a man and 'Atulongolongo named him, Kohai ("Who?").

The bottom piece also turned into a man, and he was named, Koau ("Me").

'Atulongolongo felt a small piece of the worm wriggling on his beak. He shook it off and it became a third man that he called, Momo ("Fragment").

Maui brought the men wives from Lalotonga and these three couples became the ancestors of the Tongan people.

"I knew there was potential for greatness in that ocean," Tangaloa said.

MAUI - PASIFIKA SUPERHERO

Tangaloa's brother, Maui, set off to find more land. He came to Manu'a in Samoa, where he met an elderly man named Tongataumāta'u (Tonga the expert fisherman).

Tonga showed Maui his collection of supernatural fish hooks.

"You can have any of these hooks that you want," he said.

To Tonga's surprise, Maui didn't pick one of the newly polished, intricately carved hooks. Instead, he chose a rusted old hook covered in dead leaves and spider webs.

"What can I give you in return for the hook?" Maui said.

"I don't want anything, it's a gift," Tonga replied. "But the first island that you raise, call it by my name."

Maui threw his line and hook into the ocean where the water was a light colour. He felt the hook grab onto something and pulled with all his might.

An island rose to the surface and Maui called it Tonga just as he had promised.

He also fished up some of the islands in the Ha'apai and Vava'u groups, as well as some islands in Fiji and Samoa.

KING GEORGE TUPOU I

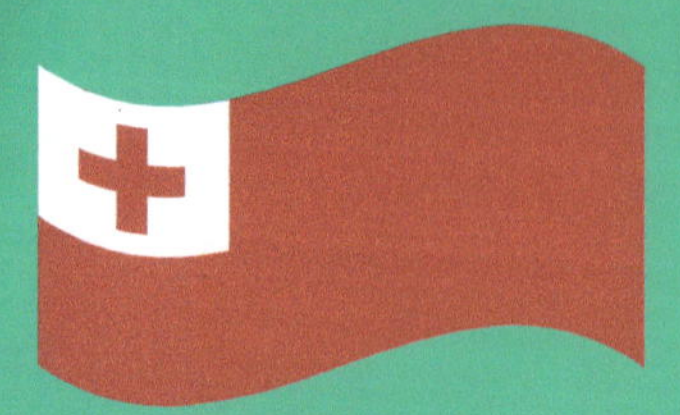

(1798-1893)
Monarch

Tonga had mostly been a peaceful place throughout history because it had been ruled by one king – the Tu'i Tonga and his descendants.

But from the late 1770s, Tonga became a divided land as three royal families tried to gain power.

The titles connected with these families were Tu'i Tonga, Tu'i Kanokupolu and Tu'i Ha'atakalaua.

One of the main people trying to take control of Tonga at this time was a man named Taufa'ahau. He was a son of the Tu'i Kanokupolu and ruled the Ha'apai islands.

Christianity was just beginning to grow in Tonga and Taufa'ahau was interested in the *lotu fo'ou* (new religion). In 1828, he visited Nuku'alofa to speak to missionaries and other Tongans who had accepted Christianity.

In 1829, he accepted Christ into his life and then persuaded 'Ulukalala of Vava'u and his people to become Christians as well.

When 'Ulukalala died in 1833, he named Taufa'ahau as his successor. Taufa'ahau was now Tu'i Ha'apai and Tu'i Vava'u
– King of Ha'apai and Vava'u.

A Christian revival took place in Vava'u in 1834, and spread through the whole of Tonga. The revival was known as Toe 'Ofa (the outpouring of God's love) and changed Taufa'ahau's thoughts about life and leadership.

From this point Taufa'ahau tried to bring peace and unity to Tonga.

In 1839, with the help of British advisors, he created written laws for his people called the Vava'u Code.

In 1845, Taufa'ahau's uncle died and he became Tu'i Kanokupolu. Now he was King over all of Tonga. He changed his name to King George Tupou I because he admired King George III of Britain.

In 1850, the Vava'u Code became a code of laws for all of Tonga.

King George wanted Tongans to have the same knowledge and wealth that Europeans had. He believed the way to achieve this was through education and so he made primary school compulsory for all Tongan children.

In 1854, King George visited Australia, a beautiful but troubled young country. He was shocked to see people begging on the streets of Sydney.

"Why aren't they growing their own food?" he asked his guide.

"Because they have no land," the guide replied.

"No Tongan will ever be humiliated like this," King George vowed.

King George passed a new code of laws in 1862. One of the laws was called the Emancipation Edict. Before this, commoners had to give food and labour freely to chiefs. The new law ended this duty and gave every Tongan the right to farm land.

Tonga prospered under King George's leadership – hundreds of children learned to read and write and understand maths; businesses thrived; farmers learned how to grow food to sell; and people's health improved.

Powerful nations like France, Germany, Great Britain and the United States were active in the Pacific during this time. They wanted to make friendships with Pacific countries so they could have more influence in the area.

King George and the important chiefs of Tonga met at Pouono in Vava'u to discuss this.

"Maybe we should get a European power to protect us from the other powers," said one of the chiefs and many of the others agreed with him.

The King had the last word. "There is a God in heaven who is King of Kings and Lord of Lords," he said. "I would like Tonga to be protected, but only by God."

He knelt down, gathered a handful of soil and threw it into the air. "God our Father, I offer to you my land and my people," he prayed.

This symbolic dedication is known as Tuku Fonua ki Langi and is regarded as one of the most special moments in Tongan history.

In 1875, King George presented a Constitution that declared Tonga would never be taken over by an outside power. He made treaties with world powers and they agreed to recognise and respect Tonga as an independent nation.

TUKU FONUA KI LANG!

King George chose the motto of Tonga: Ko e 'Otua mo Tonga ko hoku Tofi'a (God and Tonga are my inheritance). He also chose symbols to represent the nation:

FLAG:
- red - the blood of Jesus
- white – purity
- the cross – Christianity is central to life as a Tongan

ANTHEM:
"Almighty God, You are our Lord and sure defence, we put our trust in You."

SILA (Seal):
- a crown and three swords – the three royal lines (Tu'i Tonga, Tu'i Ha'atakalaua, Tu'i Kanokupolu)
- three stars – the three island groups (Tongatapu, Vava'u, Ha'apai)
- dove, olive branch, cross – Christian symbols
- ifi leaves – symbolise humility and forgiveness

KOE 'OTUA
MO TONGA KO HOKU
TOFI'A

VALERIE ADAMS

(1984-)
Olympic athlete

Village: Houma

Valerie Adams is one of the most dominant athletes in sports history. She's won multiple world championships and Olympic gold medals in her favoured event, the shot put.

She may be world famous now, but Valerie was a gentle, shy person at school. One day a bully threatened her and Valerie's "bodyguard", a much shorter girl named Erica, stood in front of her and took the punch.

Valerie may not have been a fighter on the streets, but she was when it came to athletics. In Year Nine, she went to a regional tournament and broke a twenty year old shot put record … wearing jandals!

Valerie's PE teacher encouraged her to join an athletics club so she could improve as an athlete. Valerie still remembers her first day at training. "It was scary coming from South Auckland and getting this white person to train you," she says. "I was shy about meeting someone new. I was thinking, 'How am I going to do all this training?'"

As well as training and keeping up with her schoolwork, Valerie was looking after her mum Lilika, who was sick with cancer. Lilika passed away in September 2000, during the Sydney Olympics, and Valerie promised she would try her to best to become an Olympian and make her mum proud.

In December 2000, Valerie went to the New Zealand College Games. She won the discus, hammer throw and shot put titles. She was on the way to achieving the promise she made to her mum.

Valerie qualified for the 2004 Olympics in Athens but was affected by illness and finished in ninth place. While deeply disappointed, Valerie could be proud of the fact she was only nineteen at the time. Most shot putters peak in their late twenties.

In 2008, Valerie became the first Tongan in history to win an Olympic gold medal.

In 2007, Valerie lost her dad Sidney to cancer. She went to the 2007 world championships not long after and used the inspiration of her parents' memory to become world champion for the first time.

Valerie went to the 2008 Olympics as one of the favourites to win the gold medal. Her first throw was 20.56m. No other competitor could match it. Valerie was the first Tongan in history to win an Olympic gold medal!

In 2012, Valerie defended her Olympic title in London, England. She threw 20.70m in the final, but her rival from Belarus threw 21.36m. It was the first time she'd beaten Valerie in two years. A few days after the event the Belarusian athlete was disqualified for taking banned steroids. The gold medal was awarded to Valerie.

Valerie doesn't have to cheat to win. "I do it clean," she says. "I'm doing it on potatoes, meat and veges."

A special medal ceremony was organised for Valerie when she got home. The New Zealand Governor General, Sir Jerry Mateparae, draped the gold medal around her neck. "You are the woman's shot put champion of the 30th Olympiad," he said as the audience cheered.

In 2014, Valerie was named world athlete of the year by the International Association of Athletics Federations (IAAF). She's the first female thrower in history to receive the award.

Valerie achieved another first in 2014, when she became the first woman from her village to be appointed a matāpule (chief). She was given the title name, Tongi Tupe Oe Taua. "It's unusual for a female," Valerie admitted. "If it motivates Tongan people to live healthy lives, then why not?" Valerie's title was presented to her by the Minister of Sport in Tonga, Lord Vaea.

Valerie is a proud Tongan who goes back to the kingdom often and enjoys coaching and mentoring young people in the islands.

She comes from a talented sporting family – her youngest brother Steven plays basketball for the Oklahoma City Thunder. He was the first Tongan to play in the NBA, the best basketball competition in the world.

PAEA: A MAN OUTSIDE OF THE BOX

Paea Wolfgram was Tonga's first successful Olympic athlete. He represented Tonga at the 1996 Olympic Games in Atlanta. "Looking up at Muhammad Ali as he handled the Olympic flame, I felt these Olympics would be different for Tonga," Paea said. Indeed they were. Paea won a silver medal in boxing, the first medal won by a Pacific Island nation at an Olympic Games. The man he lost to in the final was future world heavyweight champion, Vladimir Klitschko.

HIS BROTHER'S KEEPER

Seketoa was a young man who lived on Niuatoputapu island with his parents and older brother, Moimoi.

For some reason, all his life Moimoi was jealous of his younger brother. Was it because Seketoa was his parent's favourite? Was Seketoa a better fisherman than him? Did he have more friends than Moimoi?

Seketoa never understood why his brother felt that way because he never did anything to provoke him. Still, as the years went by, Moimoi's jealousy grew so strong that it turned into hate.

One day, Moimoi sent messengers to bring Seketoa to his fale. Something in Seketoa's spirit told him to be careful.

When he got to Moimoi's fale, he decided not to go in, but sat on the ground outside with his legs crossed and his head bowed in respect.

"Come inside," Moimoi called.

The sinister tone of Moimoi's voice made Seketoa even more uncomfortable. It was the same way he felt whenever he was alone with his brother as they were growing up.

"Tell me what you want me to do and I'll do it," Seketoa said.

"I want you to come inside," Moimoi repeated.

"I'm sorry my brother, I can't do that," Seketoa said.

Moimoi reached behind his back where a heavy wooden club lay hidden. He picked up the club and threw it at Seketoa.

Seketoa watched in horror as the club cartwheeled towards him. He ducked as it whistled past his ears and thundered into a tree.

Without thinking, Seketoa jumped to his feet, grabbed the club and raised it threateningly in the air. His whole body shook in a mixture of fear, shock, anger and betrayal.

"Why do you hate me so much?!" he shouted.

Moimoi stared blankly at Seketoa, waiting for him to throw the club and put him out of his misery.

"Just do what you want to me," Moimoi said, flopping dejectedly onto the floor of his fale.

At that moment Seketoa felt great sadness for his older brother.

"All I ever did was love you," he said, laying the club in the dirt. "But I can see there's something wrong with the way you feel about yourself. There's only one solution to this … It's best for me to leave our village."

Seketoa began to walk away, then stopped and looked back at Moimoi.

"Just do this one thing," he said. "Look after our parents."

Seketoa promised the people of Niuatoputapu that he would protect them and then he walked into the lagoon.

When he reached the reef, he dived into the depths and transformed into a shark.

Now he patrols the lagoons of his island, guarding the people from poisonous snakes and other sea creatures that could hurt them.

If fishermen are lost at sea at night, Seketoa helps them find the way back by lighting an underwater path with mystical lights that shine up from the ocean floor.

If a chief wants to talk to Seketoa, his matāpule (spokesmen) throw a kava root into the sea as a gift. Some small fish and sharks will come to the kava root first. They are Seketoa's matāpule. Then a big shark will come – the people believe this big shark is Seketoa.

SEKETOA AND THE SAMOAN GHOSTS

As well as guarding the sea around his island, Seketoa also protects its natural features.

One day some ghosts came from Samoa and stole a mountain from Niuatoputapu.

Seketoa ordered his matāpule to chase the ghosts and crow like roosters. The crowing would make the ghosts think it was morning and they would flee, leaving the mountain behind.

But Seketoa's plan backfired - the crowing didn't make the Samoan ghosts drop the mountain, it made them drag it faster!

"Okay I'm gonna have to do this myself," Seketoa said.

He swam underneath the ghosts and rolled over on to his back, revealing his red anus. The ghosts looked down and thought the red circle was the sun rising! They panicked and flew away leaving the stolen mountain behind.

The island called Tafahi, is the mountain abandoned by the Samoan ghosts.

QUEEN SALOTE TUPOU III 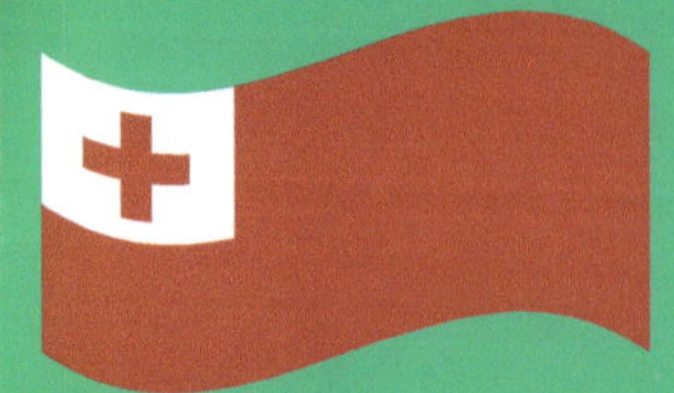

Queen Salote is one of the most beloved leaders the Pacific has known. She was born Salote Mafile'o Pilolevu on 13 March, 1900. Her father was King George Tupou II and her mother was Lavinia Veiongo, a descendant of the last Tu'i Tonga.

Salote's mother was very sick and died not long after Salote's birth. From that time she was tutored by Lesieli Tonga, the first woman to graduate from Tupou College. Lesieli and her sister Sela, taught Salote how to read, write and understand maths. They also taught her about Tongan culture and history.

In 1910, Salote went to Auckland for primary schooling and in 1913, she enrolled at Diocesan School for Girls. Her name on the enrolment form was recorded as "Charlotte Mafileo, Princess of Tonga. Father's occupation: King of Tonga."

Salote enjoyed history and English but refused to do some of the PE exercises because she didn't think they were respectful for a princess to do.

On weeknights she boarded at the school. On some weekends and in the holidays she stayed at the homes of her palangi school friends. Sometimes these families took her out to see plays, the orchestra and other types of entertainment.

When she was fifteen, Salote's family brought her back to Tonga to receive a "Tongan" education. She enjoyed listening to the old chiefs sitting around the kava bowl telling stories. Traditional punake (composers of poetry, music and dance) taught her the techniques of classical Tongan art forms.

Salote began to compose songs herself. One of her most famous compositions is a poem called Loka Siliva (The Silver Lock), a love song she wrote for Viliami Tungī Mailefihi, the man her family had arranged for her to marry.

Salote and Tungī married when Salote was seventeen years old. Tungī was expected to be the perfect husband for Salote because he was older, educated and came from a royal family line too.

In 1918, Salote experienced great joy as she became pregnant for the first time. She also endured great sadness when her father died. Suddenly, she had to learn how to be Queen, without parents to help her. Though there were lots of people around, Salote felt great loneliness.

"Who's looking after you?" one of her family asked.

"Everyone and no one," she replied. "There's no one person to talk to."

On the morning of her coronation, Salote opened her Bible and read Psalm 23. More than ever she would rely on God to be her shepherd and help her through this momentous time.

It's said that the ta'ovala Salote wore at her coronation was over 600 years old. It had been worn by her high ranking ancestors through some of the most dramatic times in Tonga's history.

Salote faced her first dramatic moment as Queen in 1918 when an influenza epidemic hit Tonga. The disease killed ten percent of the population, including members of Salote's extended family.

What an overwhelming year for Salote: married at a young age; pregnant with her first child; her father passed away; she became Queen of Tonga; and her nation experienced a major catastrophe ... No wonder she leaned so closely on God.

Some of Tonga's chiefs doubted this inexperienced teenager could lead the country. They were worried that a foreign country like Britain might try to take over and some even wanted to dethrone her and set up a new system of government.

But Salote knew her weaknesses, listened to her advisors and got to work making positive changes in Tonga. She united the two main churches, helped establish a Pacific medical school in Fiji and started a Teachers Training College.

Queen Salote as a child.

In 1926, she established Queen Salote College so girls could get a quality education and have a say in the future of Tonga. She also encouraged women to use traditional crafts like ngatu and weaving as a way to earn income for their families.

Salote loved the arts and formed a drama club, Hengihengi 'a Tonga (The Dawn of Tonga) that performed Tongan legends. She composed poetry and dances and many of her poems and songs are still heard in Tonga today. "Queen Salote is one of the greatest literary artists Tonga has produced," said Professor Futa Helu.

She formed the Tongan Traditions Committee to research and look after Tongan culture. "The customs of a people are its heritage," she often said. "I wish that all Tongans should realize the importance of full knowledge of our traditions."

She also believed in the importance of education. She built new schools and established scholarships for students to study overseas. Tonga now has one of the highest rates of PhDs in the world.

The Department of Health, a Land Court, a Savings Bank and the Tongan court system were set up during her reign. At first she used overseas experts to run these organisations, but whenever she could, she replaced them with Tongan graduates.

In 1936, her son died of rheumatic fever and in 1941, her husband Tungī died suddenly after a heart attack. These were terrible tragedies for Salote. "I'm the only one here to meet this great wave and it seems I'm going to drown," she said.

But she didn't drown; she leaned even closer to God and fought hard to overcome challenges in her personal life so that she could serve her people. "You lay down obligations only in the grave," she said.

Maybe that's why Queen Salote had such empathy for others who were suffering. She sent gifts to widows, to the sick and to the elderly; she visited the families of prisoners; and she supported nuns in their work helping people. "The real essence of being useful is the love within," she said. "With love you can serve people and be useful."

Salote cared greatly for the Tongan people and wanted to know how they felt about things. Sometimes she went out in disguise at night so she could listen to what people were saying about life in Tonga.

In 1965, Queen Salote was diagnosed with cancer and she passed away on 16 December in Auckland.

Many people believe there will never be another leader as loved by the Tongan people as Queen Salote was.

LOKA SILIVA BY QUEEN SALOTE

He māhina si'ene halani
Huelo ha 'ihe loto tahi
Langa noa hoku 'atamai
Manatu 'o fakatupu tangi
Uisa he fāhina si'ene hopo
He fihinga maile laumomo
Ko hoto kahoa tukuloto
Teu lava 'o 'ikai ke to'o
Lose moto he taukakapa
'Oku fotu he ngoue kakala
'Oku ha he seti ne tapa
Ho 'imisi koula tokotaha
'Amusia pe 'a e matangi na
'Oku ne angi fa'itehila
Kae hopoate pe kita
He 'ofa 'oku loka siliva

THE SILVER LOCK

Dear moon lighting up the sky
Its rays luminous on the sea
Bringing pain to my thoughts
And tearful memories.
Alas the fragrant fāhina is ripening
Within the tangle of maile leaves
It is my garland under cover
And I shall wear it eternally.
How heavy is that wind that blows
I am truly a slave
Clasped in the silver lock of love.

Queen Salote inspecting her soldiers.

Doctor

Village: Hunga, Vava'u

Dr Viliami Tangi is a pioneering doctor who has dedicated his life to improving the health of Tongans.

Viliami grew up on a small island in Vava'u and he says that he never dreamed that he could be a doctor one day. The island was so isolated that there was no electricity and no running water. "It seemed impossible for someone like me to be a doctor," he said.

He went to the Mission School in Nuku'alofa for his secondary schooling and impressed his teachers so much that he was offered a scholarship to study to be a doctor.

Viliami completed a Diploma in Medicine and Surgery from the Fiji School of Medicine. He returned to Tonga and from 1973 to 1978 served the Tongan people in clinics across the island group, including Niuatoputapu.

After spending time with a surgeon, Viliami decided he wanted to be a surgeon too. He went to New Zealand to study, the first Tongan doctor to go overseas and become a specialist. It was important that Viliami did well. "If I was successful, more would follow," he said.

When he graduated he returned to Tonga as the only qualified surgeon in the hospital. His specialty was General Surgery and included burns, children's health, trauma and rural work.

He worked at Vaiola hospital for ten years, then moved with his family to Griffith, New South Wales to start his own practise. He became a respected and successful doctor in Australia.

One day in 1999, Viliami received a phone call from the Prime Minister of Tonga. "You've been appointed Minister of Health," he said. "The King wants you to come home so that you can start next week."

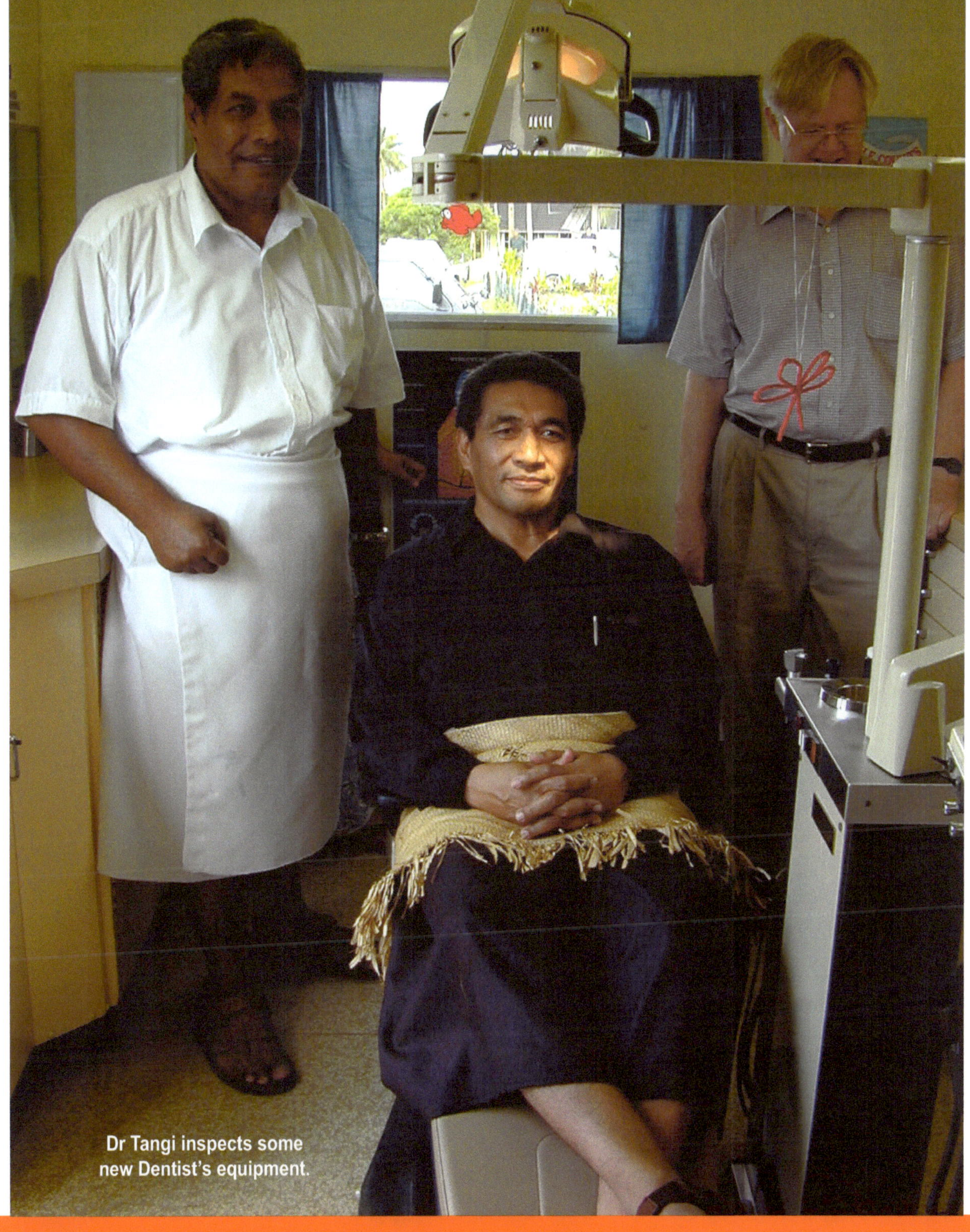

Dr Tangi inspects some new Dentist's equipment.

What a challenge for Viliami. His four children were settled in school and university and the family were happy living in Australia, running their thriving health clinic. But he couldn't say no to the King!

"No one in the history of Tonga has turned down a thing like that and I didn't want to be the first," he said. Viliami's family agreed that moving back to Tonga was the right thing to do.

The first big job he was given was to renovate Vaiola hospital. Viliami had other important projects too. He wanted to increase the number of doctors in Tonga. And he wanted to improve some of the main health issues in the islands including infant mortality, maternal mortality, diet, physical exercise, smoking, life expectancy and water supply.

In 2006, His Majesty King Taufa'ahau Tupou IV appointed Viliami, Deputy Prime Minister of Tonga. He has held other positions in the government including Acting Minister of Police, Prison and Fire Services.

But medicine remained his first love and while an active member of the Tongan parliament, he continued to work as a surgeon whenever he could. "There is an understanding in Cabinet that if I'm not there, I am operating," he said.

From 2005 to 2007, Viliami served on the Executive Board of the World Health Organisation (WHO). Viliami's membership in such a group indicates how significant his contribution has been to health, especially in Tonga and the Pacific.

Viliami and his team have brought tremendous improvements to health in Tonga: the hospital has been renovated; there are twice as many doctors as when he first began and many of the important goals he set have been achieved through the work of Tonga Health.

In 2008, he was awarded the Knight Grand Cross of the Royal Order of Queen Salote in recognition of his work.

"I'm a firm believer in faith and many's the time I've knelt down and asked for help and direction," Viliami said. "There is no doubt in my mind that God has played a major role in my journey."

A POET DOCTOR

Dr Karlo Mila is an award-winning poet and medical professional who specialises in mental health. Karlo is of Tongan, Samoan and European descent and identifies with the villages of Kolofo'ou and Ofu. She attended Tonga High School as a teenager.

Much of Karlo's research and work focuses on the health of Pacific young people.

"Being Tongan is being proud of who you are, where you come from, who you are connected to and how you belong," Karlo says.

"Being Tongan connects to you a very rich heritage, a rich history of great kings and queens, a huge empire of influence that spans far beyond Tonga's borders, very powerful values, a beautiful material culture, incredible people and a special land."

Karlo represented Tonga at the Cultural Olympiad London, 2012.

Representing Tonga on the Executive Board of the World Health Organisation.

THE FIRST TU'I TONGA

Seketoa was a chief who lived in Niuatoputapu. He had a daughter named Ilaheva who was very beautiful. Seketoa didn't want her to marry any of the men on his island, so he sent her in a canoe with some of his warriors to look for a husband in the neighbouring islands of Tonga.

As Vava'u emerged in the distance, the perspiring warriors cheered knowing that it wouldn't be long before they could get back to their families on Niuatoputapu.

"Okay, here you go, there should be a good husband for you here," they said attempting to usher Ilaheva out of the canoe.

"Ah, no, I'm not going ashore here," she replied firmly. "There's too many mountains on that island. I don't like climbing mountains."

The warriors groaned, placed Ilaheva carefully back in her seat and began paddling again. At last, the Ha'apai islands came into view.

"Okay, no mountains here, bye bye," the exhausted warriors said, lifting Ilaheva out of the canoe.

"No mountains but I don't like the look of that," she said pointing to a flume of ash and smoke rising out of a nearby volcano.

The warriors reluctantly lifted Ilaheva back into the canoe and paddled way from Vava'u. Finally, they came to Tongatapu.

"No mountains, no volcanoes, perfect," they said, briskly carrying Ilaheva to shore.

"But what am I going to eat? Where am I going to sleep?" she called.

"Ask your new husband," the warriors replied as they paddled quickly away.

Ilaheva didn't know anyone on this island and felt scared. She ate some shellfish along the shore and when night came she hid in the forest.

Tangaloa 'Eitumatupu'a saw Ilaheva from his home in the sky and felt sorry for her. He climbed down a toa tree and introduced himself to her. After a while Ilaheva and 'Eitumatupu'a became close and Ilaheva became pregnant.

'Eitumatupu'a went back to his home in the sky before the child, a boy, was born. Ilaheva named the boy Aho'eitu.

"Who is my dad?" Aho'eitu asked Ilaheva one day.

"His name is Tangaloa 'Eitumatupu'a and he lives in the sky," Ilaheva explained.

"I want to go and meet him."

Ilaheva rubbed coconut oil on his skin, wrapped tapa around his waist and combed his hair. She showed him the toa tree and Aho'eitu began climbing.

When he reached the top of the tree, Aho'eitu saw a road stretching across the sky. He followed the road until he came to a man gardening.

"Have you seen my father?" the boy asked. "His name is Tangaloa 'Eitumatupu'a."

The man lay his gardening tools on the ground and looked intently into the boy's eyes. Warm tears rolled down his cheeks.

"I'm your father," he said and they embraced each other, weeping.

"You have some brothers too," 'Eitumatupu'a said. "Would you like to meet them? They're playing sika not far from here."

Aho'eitu found his brothers and introduced himself. Sadly, his brothers were anything but welcoming.

"Who does this guy think he is, coming here and trying to take Dad's attention?" they whispered. They were so angry and thoughtless that they lost control of their feelings and killed Aho'eitu. They cut off his head and threw it into a bush where no one would find it. Then they ate his body.

"Where's my son?" 'Eitumatupu'a asked when they returned home later that day.

The repentant brothers admitted what they had done and 'Eitumatupu'a ordered them to bring Aho'eitu's head to him. He put the head into a wooden bowl and told his sons to vomit into it. Then he covered the bowl with leaves.

"Stand guard around the bowl," he commanded.

After a while, a miracle took place inside that bowl - the body of Aho'eitu re-formed and came back to life. Aho'eitu emerged from the bowl and smiled at his brothers.

"I don't know why you did that to me," he said. "But I want you to know I forgive you." Then he hugged each of the brothers in turn. He was a forgiving person just like his grandfather Seketoa.

Soon it was time for Aho'eitu to return home to Tongatapu. 'Eitumatupu'a instructed his brothers to go with him, to protect him and his family.

This is how Aho'eitu became the first Tu'i Tonga (King of Tonga) and every Tu'i Tonga since then traces their descent through him.

WARRIORS COME OUT TO PLAY

The story of Aho'eitu includes a reference to a game called sika. Here are some other ancient Tongan games as recorded by William Mariner (see Notes section):

LIANGI

Two players sit opposite each other, each holding five small sticks in their left hand. A player begins the game by making one of three hand signs: an open hand, a closed hand or a pointing index finger. The opponent makes a sign at the same time. If the opponent makes the same sign, then it's his/her turn to lead. If the opponent does not make the same sign then the lead player makes another sign. If this happens five times in a row, the lead player drops one stick. The other player takes a turn to lead. Whichever player drops their five sticks first wins the game. If there's an argument, the game is decided by a wrestling match!

TOLO

A six foot high post is planted in the ground. A piece of soft wood is tied on the top of the post. Players try to throw a spear into the soft wood. There are two teams of six to eight players. Each player has three throws. The winning team is the one with the most spears stuck in the wood at the end.

HIKO

Hiko is a juggling game only played by females. The players juggle tuitui nuts, usually four or five nuts at one time. One legend says the record for the number of nuts juggled is ten! There is even a Hiko Tau'olunga dance. The players chant poetry as they juggle.

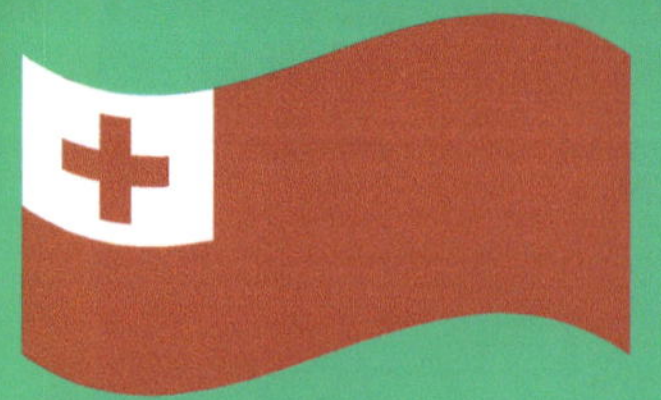

Evangelist

Tonga is one of the most spiritual nations in the world: churches can be seen in every village, there are strict rules about behaviour on the Sabbath and even the national flag proclaims that Tonga is a Christian country.

In the middle of the eighteenth century, a Christian revival swept through England. People were hungry to experience what it really meant to be a Christian and to share the gospel with those who hadn't heard it before.

A group of people formed the London Missionary Society (LMS) and in 1797, ten missionaries were sent to Tonga.

The LMS missionaries settled at Hihifo on Tongatapu, but they weren't able to bring the change they hoped for. Tongans were interested in the clothing, iron goods and other items the foreigners brought with them. But they weren't interested in their religion.

There was much warfare between chiefs in Tonga at this time and three of the missionaries were killed. The others fled on a passing whaling ship in January 1800.

In 1826, the Wesleyan Missionary Society sent John Hutchinson and John Thomas to Tonga to see if they could do better. But like the LMS before them, the Wesleyans struggled to gain acceptance and the mission almost closed.

The work was saved when a new group of missionaries arrived in 1828, including the experienced Nathaniel Turner who had worked with the Maori in New Zealand.

Nathaniel was more respectful and sensitive to Tongan culture than previous missionaries had been and he managed to begin a small fellowship in Nuku'alofa.

The first public baptism service took place in Nuku'alofa on 4 January, 1829.

Seven young men were baptised and each one received a Biblical name to go with his Tongan name: Mafile'o (Noa), Takanoe (Moses), Lauola ('Ilaisa), Kavamoelolo (Panepasa), Lavemai (Siosifa), Mou'ngaevale (Sione) and Vi (Pita).

"They are the first fruits of a most glorious harvest eventually to be gathered in these islands," said John Thomas.

After the baptism, each man stood and explained why he had accepted Christ. Many of them spoke of how commoners were said to have no souls in traditional Tongan religion and only chiefs went to Pulotu to live forever in paradise. It was believed that when commoners died, their bodies merely rotted away.

The first converts loved Christianity's message that everyone is equal in God's eyes and that everyone has the opportunity to live in paradise after death, not just those who have high status.

The missionaries built a school in Nuku'alofa and taught people how to read and write so they could study the Bible for themselves.

One of the most influential of the new converts was Pita Vi, one of the King's fishermen.

In October 1829, Taufa'ahau asked the missionaries to send a teacher with him to Ha'apai so he could learn more about Christianity. The missionaries wanted Tongans to lead the work of the mission, so they sent Pita and his wife, Litia.

Evangelism could be dangerous as many parts of Tonga were not Christianised and were opposed to the lotu fo'ou (new religion).

On the evening before the historic journey, the missionaries held a prayer meeting for Pita and Litia.

"Your profession is like that of your namesake, a fisherman," John Thomas said. "God grant that you too may catch men for Christ." Then he prayed a blessing over the couple, the first Tongan Bible teachers.

They supplied them with portions of the Bible, alphabet cards, books to teach reading, pens and writing paper.

As the group were sailing to Ha'apai, Taufa'ahau saw a white shark swimming ahead. He believed it was the shark god, Taufalahi.

Taufa'ahau decided to test the powers of the lotu fo'ou.

"Pita Vi, if the God you believe in is true, he can save you from that shark," he said. "But if Taufalahi eats you, then the gods I believe in are true." Then he told his men to throw Pita in the ocean.

Taufa'ahau sailed away, leaving Pita in the shark infested waters.

Later that day Taufa'ahau was about to begin a kava ceremony when a voice called out that a man was walking out of the sea! The man walked up the beach, quietly entered the fale and sat next to Taufa'ahau in the kava circle.

It was Pita Vi.

"Well done Pita," said Taufa'ahau. "Your God is indeed powerful and the true God."

Taufa'ahau accepted the Christian teachings he learned from Pita and Litia and encouraged all his people in Ha'apai to do the same. Then he and Pita travelled to Vava'u and taught their king, 'Ulukalala and his people the gospel too.

Later in their lives, Pita and Litia were one of four couples who volunteered to go to Samoa to begin a mission there. The mission became known in Samoa as the Lotu Toga (church from Tonga).

"Love in their hearts had led them to offer themselves and enabled them to give up their friends and homes in Tonga," said John Thomas.

Thanks to Pita, Litia and other early Tongan missionaries, the Christian gospel spread throughout Tonga and the Pacific.

(1984-)
American football player

Haloti Ngata is one of the most successful Tongan players in the history of the National Football League (NFL). He's won a Superbowl, been to five Pro Bowls, and in his prime was regarded as one of the best defensive players in the game.

Haloti's parents, Solomone and Olga, migrated from Tonga to the United States in the early 1970s and met at a dance in California. They had three children.

Haloti, the youngest, was named after his uncle, Haloti Moala, who played college football before he was injured and had to retire. Maybe Haloti's parents hoped their little boy would follow in his uncle's footsteps.

The family moved to Salt Lake City, Utah and Haloti attended Highland High School. He played rugby for the school but his goal was to play American football just like his namesake. Haloti even carried a photo of his uncle around with him. On the back of the photo he wrote, "This is my uncle Haloti. He didn't make it to the NFL, but I will."

Haloti's dad was a hard worker who didn't like to see his children lying around. But Haloti loved to sleep when he was young. One day Haloti was drifting into an afternoon nap when he heard his father walking down the hall.

"Haloti!" Dad called. "Where are you? You better not be sleeping again boy!"

Haloti quickly transformed from sleeping to doing push ups. "Good boy son," Dad said as he came into the room. "That's how you'll achieve your dreams in life, by being a hard worker."

The family was very religious and weren't allowed to watch TV on Sundays ... well most Sundays. "'The only time we could watch TV on a Sunday was when the Superbowl was on," Haloti laughs. Little did he know that one day he would be playing in the Superbowl himself.

After leaving school, Haloti went to Oregon University to play college football. He became one of the best players in America. Tackles, sacks, blocked kicks, Haloti did it all. "He has the size/speed ratio that makes him a physical freak," said his coach.

In 2002, Haloti's father died in an accident while driving his truck. Haloti was devastated. "Why did you do this to me?" he asked God. "Why did you take my best friend?" But there were no answers. Haloti found it hard to focus and says he lost his faith, and his motivation for football and school.

The following year, he suffered a knee injury that ended his season. Haloti was so discouraged he felt like quitting and going home to Utah. Fortunately he had great teammates who supported him through those challenging times, especially his best friend, Matt Toeaina.

After a while Haloti regained his faith. He realised that life is challenging for everyone. He taped pictures of his dad to his wall and promised him he would be the best player he could be.

Haloti achieved the dream
he had as a child when he
made the NFL in 2006.

Meanwhile, Haloti's mum Olga was struggling with her health. The NFL dream became even more important to Haloti so he could pay for the medical help she needed.

Sadly, while Haloti was preparing for the NFL Draft, his mum passed away. Haloti was determined to respond better than he had when his dad died. "I started thanking God that I had both of them in my life," he said. "Knowing that they were proud of me has helped me move forward."

Haloti achieved his dream when the Baltimore Ravens selected him in the 2006 NFL Draft. The Ravens were so desperate to get Haloti that they traded two players for him. One of the first people he hugged was uncle Haloti.

Haloti knew the real hard work was about to begin. But that was okay, he'd learned all about hard work from his dad. He worked so hard and played so well in his first year that he was named to the All Rookie team.

The Ravens became one of the best defensive teams in the NFL and many people say that Haloti was a major reason for that. In 2009, he was voted to the Pro Bowl – meaning he was now one of the best players in the NFL.

In 2013, Haloti played in the Superbowl against the San Francisco 49ers. The Ravens won the game 34-31 and Haloti played a major part with his defensive work and important tackles.

Haloti is also known for the work he does off the field. He began the Haloti Ngata Family Foundation to help struggling families. He gives gifts to needy people and visits children in orphanages because he knows what it's like to lose your parents. He also runs projects to raise awareness of diabetes.

Haloti's parents would definitely be proud of the way their son is living the values they taught him and his siblings as a child.

TONGANS ON THE GRID IRON

The first Tongan to play in the NFL was Vai Sikahema. Vai was a running back and kick returner who played eight seasons for the Green Bay Packers and Philadelphia Eagles. Vai was born in Nuku'alofa.

Ma'ake and Chris Kemoeatu are Tongan brothers who have both won Superbowls. Ma'ake played Nose Tackle for the Ravens, while Chris played Offensive Guard and won two Superbowls with the Pittsburgh Steelers.

Star Lotulelei played for the Carolina Panthers in the 2016 Superbowl.

THE LEGEND OF THE SCAR FACED ORPHAN HERO

Motukuveevalu and Kae lived on Tongatapu at a time when a cannibal named Pungalotohoa terrorised the island. Motu sent his pregnant wife to safety in Ha'apai while he fled to the bush with other men to make a plan to destroy Punga.

Some of Motu's enemies recognised Kae and killed her. They tore her unborn child from her womb and threw him into the ocean. Miraculously, the child survived and washed up on a beach near Lafonga.

Birds pecked at the baby's face causing terrible scarring. An old couple rescued the baby from the birds and named him Munimatamahae. Muni was the name of the beach, matamahae means scarred face.

The old couple took Muni home and looked after him and he grew to become one of the strongest and most talented young men in the village. But some chiefs mistreated Muni because he looked different with his scarred face. They were determined to send him back to where he came from, wherever that was.

One day, they gave him a seemingly impossible task. "You must weave half of a fishing net, while the rest of the village weaves the other half," a spokesmen announced. "If we finish our half before you finish yours, you have to leave."

"That's not fair," Muni's elderly father said. "There are so many more of you."

"Oh you're right," said the spokesman. "Okay to make it fairer … you and your wife can help him!"

"It's okay, Dad," Muni said. "You guys rest over there in the shade, leave it to me."

Muni started on his half of the net and to everyone's astonishment, he finished while the rest of the chiefs and people were arguing about who was sitting where!

The village council quickly met and devised another challenge.

"Think you're smart?" said the spokesman. "Try this then. You will build one half of a fence around this malae stretched out before you, while the rest of the village builds the other half. If we finish our half before you finish yours … you're outta here!"

Once again, while the rest of the village argued about who was going to get what, Muni gathered the wood and rope he needed and built his part of the fence before they'd even begun.

"Okay tough guy," the spokesman said. "Build an outrigger canoe and a shed for it. One side will be built by you and the other by the village and chiefs. If you fail … you know what happens."

Muni didn't bother to chop wood to build the shed - he simply uprooted trees and broke them into the pieces he needed. He used coconut palm fronds for the thatching on the roof.

Once again he finished his part of the task well before the rest of the workers.

"There has to be a way to get rid of this guy," the chiefs complained to each other. Suddenly one chief smiled. "I've got the ultimate plan," he whispered.

"Muni, take the village canoe to the lagoon. You and your parents are to watch over it tonight. If anything happens to the canoe … you're gone."

"What kind of challenge is that!" complained one of the chiefs.

"Trust me," he whispered, winking deviously.

That night, as Muni and his parents slept in the canoe, the chief swam quietly out and cut the rope that tied it to an anchor stick. Then he broke holes in the side of the boat. He pushed the boat from its moorings and it began to drift out to sea.

Muni woke when he felt the boat sinking, grabbed a food bowl and began scooping water out. He pulled a plank off the side of the canoe and used it to row them all to the nearest island.

Muni and his parents collapsed on the beach of the remote island, exhausted but safe. When they thought Muni was asleep, his parents gazed lovingly at him and reminisced about the special day they found him washed ashore all those years ago.

But Muni wasn't fully asleep. He sat up and asked the old couple to tell him everything they could about his birth parents. Muni wept as they told him of his mother's death and how his father was living in constant danger from a cannibal.

"I have to go and help my dad," Muni told them.

Later that day, Muni approached the area of the forest in Tongatapu where the old couple said he would find his father.

"Motu!" he called. "Motu! Are you here?"

A muscular arm reached out of the bushes and pulled Muni off the track. The arm belonged to Muni's father, Motu.

"Stop yelling," he said. "Punga will know where we are."

Muni explained who he was and his father embraced him. "It's so good to see you, son," he said. "Thank you for coming to help."

Muni woke early the next day. "Man, this forest is really uncomfortable to sleep in," he said rubbing his back. "I feel sorry for Dad. I'm gonna make him something more cozy."

He began pulling trees out of the ground and soon cleared a nice little section of the forest.

"Hey, stop that!" Motu said running to Muni. "Punga can easily see us now!"

Later that day, Muni thought he would help his dad by preparing him a meal. He lit a fire and lay some coconuts on it to roast them. But when Motu returned from fishing he ran to the fire and threw leaves on it to put it out.

"Don't light fires!" he said. "Punga will see the smoke and come and kill us."

"Man, Dad, this Punga guy has got you living in too much fear," Muni said. "You can't live like this. I'm gonna go sort him out."

"What! Hey come back, he's too strong, he's – " Motu said, but Muni was already gone.

Muni followed the smell of burning human flesh to Punga's fale. A massive gate towered above him, blocking the entrance to the fale.

"Punga, come out here, I want to talk to you!" Muni called. "Where you at?"

Muni waited but heard nothing but the sound of the distant ocean. So he ripped the huge gate apart and threw it into the forest. Inside the compound he saw a grove of gigantic kava plants. "I'll have these," he said, ripping the plants out from their roots.

Muni spotted Punga's servants hiding in the fale. "Tell Punga I did this," he said. "Tell him to come and find me if he wants them back … And if he wants a one out."

When Punga returned from hunting and saw the carnage done to his gate and his kava plants, he was furious. He chased after Muni and found him in the middle of the forest.

"I challenge you to a throwing contest," Punga said. "See who can throw this spear the furthest. If I win … you will be my dinner tonight."

Muni's spear flew into the air like a hawk. It went so far it disappeared into the sky.

"Okay, a boxing match," Punga said. "If I win … you're mine."

In an instant Muni sprang at Punga and pummelled him with kicks, elbows and punches. Then he lifted Punga's limp body over his head and slammed it down on to the ground. Punga's bones were crushed and he became coral.

The whole of Tonga rejoiced at the news of Punga's death, thankful that they could at last return to their homes. And they owed it to one of Tonga's greatest heroes, a scar faced orphan boy named Munimatamahae.

PROFESSOR 'ILAISA FUTA 'I HA'ANGANA HELU

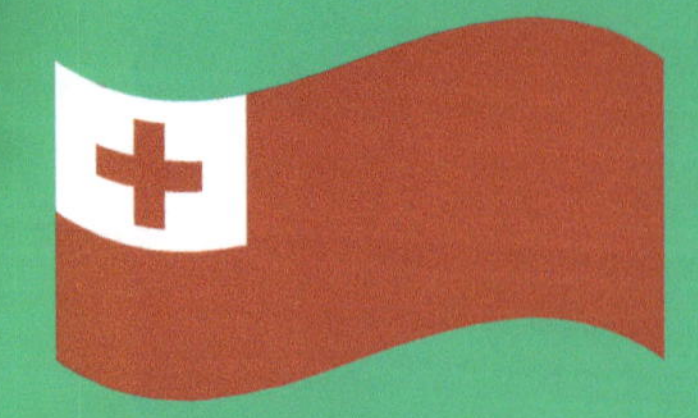

(1934-2010)
Academic

Village: Lotofoa

Futa Helu was a philosopher, teacher and writer who started a university in Tonga that became one of the most famous schools in the Pacific. He loved Tongan culture, but he also encouraged people to question it.

From an early age Futa enjoyed learning and thinking about the world. He was one of the founding students of Tonga High School and impressed his teachers with his study habits and love of knowledge.

Futa's family encouraged him to go as far as he could in education. They sold copra (dried coconut) to raise money to send him to school in Australia where he studied at Newington College and then Sydney University.

During his time in Australia, Futa learned more about western culture. He studied English literature, maths, philosophy and physics. At the same time he worked in market gardens and restaurants and mixed with people of many different cultures.

When he went home to Tonga, Futa started his own school, which he named 'Atenisi Institute. 'Atenisi is the Tongan name for Athens. Futa liked the way that ancient Greek philosophers thought about life and the world.

Students at 'Atenisi learned a combination of Tongan and western culture - opera music, Plato and Shakespeare as well as Tongan arts and history.

Futa accepted students who were rejected by other schools and taught them to believe in themselves. He made the fees as low as possible so that even very poor people could gain an education. Student families gifted mats and ngatu tapa cloth to the school to supplement the low fees.

'Atenisi 's performing arts troupe toured the world raising awareness and funds for the school.

Futa also started the 'Atenisi Foundation for the Performing Arts, an operatic troupe that toured the world raising awareness and funds for the school.

While Futa loved his culture, he also believed it was important to criticise culture sometimes. All their lives, Tongan young people were told what to do and what to think; to obey and not to question. Futa taught his students to do the opposite. He wanted them to challenge and to question.

Some people in Tongan society and the government condemned Futa's methods. They said he was teaching young people to be rebellious. But Futa didn't see it that way. He believed that encouraging young people to talk about issues would make them better citizens.

'Atenisi graduates have contributed positively to Tongan society and include business people, clergymen and university teachers.

"'Atenisi opened up my mind and now I see things clearer," one graduate told Paul Janman, director of the film, Tongan Ark. "Once you understand things, you are free."

Futa lived during a time in Tonga when many people were beginning to question the monarchy. Futa was one of those who wanted peaceful change and in the 1990s, 'Atenisi became a base for other people who felt the same.

Some people said that Futa should stay out of the King's business and respect the position of the monarchy.

"Socrates was criticised by those in authority," Futa said. "They told him to mind his own business too. They asked him, 'Why do you have to interfere?' He answered, 'I interfere because I want to participate.' That is the essence of democracy."

In 2006, frustration at the political situation in Tonga led to rioting and violence in Nuku'alofa. Six young men lost their lives in the riots. "We have to change," Futa said at the time.

The hopes of Futa and others were fulfilled in 2008, when the King agreed to reduce most of his powers.

Futa passed away in 2010 and will be remembered as one of the most inspirational teachers and thinkers Tonga has known.

TONGAN ARK

Paul Janman is a New Zealand film maker who studied at 'Atenisi and made a film about Futa called *Tongan Ark*. Here is footage of the performance and ceremony that accompanied the world premiere of *Tongan Ark* in 2012. Download a QR Code Reader app, open the app, point your device's camera at the code and enjoy.

Futa enjoying one of his favourite pastimes – reading!

EMELINE AFEAKI-MAFILE'O

(1975-)
Entrepreneur

Villages: Kolofo'ou, Ha'apai (Tonga), Falefa/ Savelalo (Samoa), Ngati Awa

Emeline was born and raised in South Auckland, New Zealand and from an early age her parents stressed two things. "We expect you to go as far as you can with your education," they said. "And to make a contribution to life."

One day, a group of girls bullied Emeline at school, calling her names and spreading stories about her. The next day, the bullies attacked Emeline without warning. "Why didn't you fight back?" her dad asked later.

"I would never do well at school if I did that, Dad," Emeline replied. She had a bigger vision than fighting.

One of her best friends at the time was a girl named Susan. Susan had serious health problems which kept her away from school a lot. Emeline was sad that her friend didn't get to experience events like the school ball and Seventh Form dinner.

After finishing high school, Emeline went to university to study Optometry. Her friend sadly passed away during this time. "I wish I could help people like Susan to have a better life," Emeline thought. That's when she decided to study Social Work.

After graduating, Emeline spent a year doing voluntary work at a school in Tonga. The teachers had very few resources but the experience showed her that you don't need much to make a difference in people's lives.

She returned to New Zealand and began a homework centre for youth and a tutoring service for adults who struggled with literacy.

"Would you come and tutor my children please?" asked a lady one evening. "They really need support with their reading and writing."

Local workers harvesting coffee beans for Emeline's coffee factory in Tonga.

Imagine Emeline's surprise when she arrived at the family garage to find sixty children patiently waiting! The woman was a pastor's wife and had invited all the children from church to come. "Wow, this is how big the need is," Emeline thought.

She thought about her grandmother, who she was named after. She always made children feel special and Emeline wanted to do that too. "My grandma has always been my inspiration," she says.

For a long time Emeline worried about the plight of young women in South Auckland, especially those involved in teen prostitution.

In 2001, she began an organisation called Affirming Women (AW) to connect these young people with female mentors who taught them how to believe in themselves and find a greater purpose for life.

The program was so successful that some agencies began to refer boys as well. So Emeline hired male mentors and changed the group's name to Affirming Works.

AW's mentoring style is based on Pacific values like community, love and respect. They call the program Tupu'anga (grow from your roots). They believe people find strength and resilience from their cultural backgrounds and the things they love.

AW mentors work with young people in schools across South Auckland. Over ninety percent of the youth they mentor complete their schooling and go on to tertiary study or fulltime work. Many are now mentors themselves. Some of the people they've helped include All Black, Charlie Faumuina and hip hop artist, Young Sid.

In 2010, Emeline and her husband 'Alipate went to Tonga to buy coffee for a café they started called Community Café. The coffee factory was for sale at the time, so they bought it, moved to Tonga, restored the factory and renamed it Tupu'anga Coffee.

They paid the farmers fair trade prices and employed locals to harvest, roast and package the coffee. Today they ship over seven hundred kilograms of coffee a month around the world! Profits are used to help fund AW's mentoring programs.

Emeline also uses her experience to advise city councils and the government. She helps them understand the best ways to work with Pacific young people and their families.

Emeline has won many awards for her work, including the Sir Peter Blake Emerging Leaders Award and a Women of Influence Award (the highest award for women in New Zealand). In 2016, she was made a Member of the New Zealand Order of Merit.

Awards are cool, but in Emeline's eyes, she's just doing what her parents and grandparents taught her to do.

"Being Tongan to me means knowing my role," she says. "When I lived in Tonga, I learned what it means to know your place in the family and the village, to know when to serve and when to be served."

She encourages young people to think the same. "As a teen it's quite easy to think of yourself but it's so empowering when you think of others," she says. "I like it when young people identify with their cultural homeland and think about helping."

"Understand who you are. Occupy your space, which means know your role and submit to it. Fulfil all the different roles you have in life as a Tongan person and that will make you happy and resilient."

ANCIENT TRADE

When Emeline and 'Alipate sell Tupu'anga Coffee around the world, they're following in the footsteps of their ancestors. In ancient times, Tongans frequently travelled to Fiji, Samoa and other Pacific islands to trade for fine mats, large canoes, pots, sandalwood and weapons. The most popular trading items included red feathers and whale's teeth.

Mentoring young people is an important part of Emeline's work.

Hina was a beautiful woman who lived at Halakakala (The Road of Flowers). Hina's parents were so protective that they put her in the middle of an enclosure surrounded by eight fences and one hundred guards!

A warrior hero named Sinilau heard about Hina's beauty and set out in a huge war canoe to find her. When he arrived he was shocked to see the amount of protection placed around her by her parents.

Sinilau stood outside the first fence with his brother wondering how he could ever get inside to see Hina. "I'm just going to jump the fence," he said finally. "If I'm not back by the morning then go home, cos I'm probably dead!"

When it was dark, Sinilau jumped the first fence. He was about to run to the next fence when he spied a guard sitting next to a fire.

"I'm sick of looking after this girl, Hina," the guard complained to himself. "Night after night, lighting fires, watching fences ... I wish I could go home to my own family."

"Pssssstttt!" Sinilau whispered.

The guard turned, his spear raised in defence.

"You want me to take your place so you can go home and see your family?"

The guard eagerly swapped places with Sinilau. As soon as he was gone, Sinilau ran to the next fence and jumped over it. Luckily the guard in this part of the enclosure was asleep and Sinilau put his fire out as he crept past. Amazingly, he found all the rest of the guards sleeping too. At last, Sinilau reached the middle of the enclosure where Hina lay sleeping.

She was wrapped in fine tapa cloth, a red hibiscus flower rested on her ear, and the coconut oil on her arms glistened in the moonlight …. Hina looked to Sinilau like a supernatural princess.

He edged closer and touched her shoulder hoping to wake her without frightening her.

"Get away from me!" Hina murmured and turned over.

Sinilau touched her shoulder again. "I said get away!" she said and kicked out with her leg.

"I didn't come all this way to give up this easy," Sinilau said to himself. He touched her shoulder a third time. This time Hina sat up, raised her fists and spat at him.

"Woooooh, what's your problem!" Sinilau said, wiping spit from his face.

"Huh? What? Who are you?" Hina said rubbing her eyes.

"Whoever said you're beautiful is right," Sinilau said. "But you are one troubled girl." He showed her the bruises her kicking had made on his legs. "You go back to sleep Hina, I'm going back to Samoa."

Sinilau was so upset about what had happened in Tonga that when he got home he demanded total silence in his village.

Hina was intrigued by this man who had come so far to find her, so she swam to Samoa to look for him. By the time she reached his village she was exhausted and lay dripping wet on the beach like a clump of seaweed.

"What are you doing here like this?" asked an old lady.

Hina explained that she had come to look for her true love, Sinilau. The woman clapped her hands.

"Sinilau is my son," she said. "He's a stubborn boy but there is something you can do to impress him." She gave Hina some oranges and taught her how to juggle them while singing.

"Who's making noise?" Sinilau questioned his servants. "Tell that person to stop."

The servants obeyed and Hina stopped performing. But just as Sinilau lay down to rest, the singing and entertainment started up again.

"Oh my gosh," he said angrily. "Do I have to do everything myself!"

He stormed down to the beach ready to punish the disobedient noise maker. But when he saw it was Hina, he fell in love with her again.

"She's too beautiful to be a human," said the other ladies in the village. "She's a spirit, you better send her into the forest."

Reluctantly, Sinilau did as the ladies said and Hina spent the next few years living on her own in a hut in the forest. One day she saw Sinilau hunting and called out to him. Sinilau was shocked to see how ragged and sad she looked.

Meanwhile, Hina's Tongan family were worried because they hadn't heard from her in a long time. Her uncle and a fleet of warriors went to Samoa to look for her.

"Why do you look like this?" her uncle asked when he found her in the forest.

"Oh um, I've been really sick," she said.

"Sinilau isn't looking after you properly," he said shaking his head. "Come on, let's go home."

Sinilau followed Hina to Tonga but her parents wouldn't allow him to see her. They placed her back in the middle of the enclosure, and doubled the amount of guards.

Now it was Sinilau's turn to be depressed. All he had to remember of Hina was her little pet dog.

One day Sinilau asked a guard to give Hina a basket of yams.

"Tell her to chew these and mash them up so I can give them to her dog," he said.

Hina did so and sent the yams back to Sinilau. But Sinilau didn't give the yams to the dog, he ate them himself. Hina's parents saw this and admired his humility. They agreed that Hina and Sinilau could now be married.

Sinilau and Hina decided to have a canoe race to celebrate their marriage. The race was fun until they found themselves drifting into a whirlpool. Sinilau called for help and a canoe came from the village to rescue them.

"Don't worry about me," Hina shouted courageously. "Help Sinilau, he's the one everyone loves."

Sinilau was saved, but brave Hina drowned in the whirlpool as her canoe was sucked under the water before the rescuers could get to her.

The whirlpool in which Hina sacrificed her life for her husband is near 'Eua and is a known meeting place for sharks. "Hina, come and get your garland of flowers," the fishermen call. When the sharks come, the fishermen throw ropes around their necks and take them back to the village to eat them.

OCEAN DEEP LOVE

There are stories about the romance of Hina and Sinilau across Polynesia. Hina is sometimes known as Sina, Ina or Hine. Sinilau is also called Tinirau, Tingilau or Kinilau. Tongans say that Sinilau lives in Samoa; Samoans say that he lives in Vava'u; and Cook Islanders say he lives on a beautiful floating island called Motutapu (Sacred Island). Professor Futa Helu believes some of the Sinilau-Hina stories have taken on aspects of the Cinderella stories of Europe.

TONGA 'HAKU' FIFITA

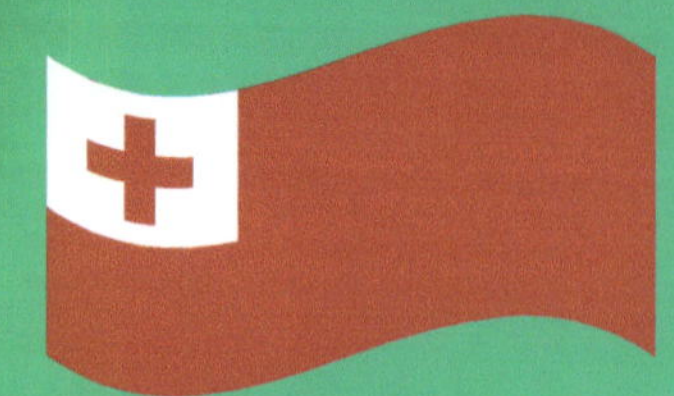

Professional wrestler

Villages: Kolomotu'a / Kolofo'ou

Tonga Fifita is a former WWF World Tag Team Champion, two time WCW Hardcore Champion and one of the most feared men in the history of pro wrestling. He fought under the names Meng (WCW), King Tonga, King Haku and Haku (WWF).

Tonga grew up in Tongatapu and attended Tonga College. When he was fourteen, some government officials came to his school to find a group of boys to study Sumo wrestling in Japan. A special assembly was called to name the lucky boys. "If I can do this Lord," Tonga prayed, "then please let me go."

After school, Tonga ran home to tell his parents he'd been selected. "That's great," his mother said. "But when you finish, I really want you to become a doctor."

While Tonga was studying in Japan, the owner of the Sumo company passed away. The business was bought by All Japan Pro Wrestling and Tonga began to learn a new form of wrestling: wrestling for entertainment. The company sent him to America to train and he wrestled all over the United States, in Canada and in Puerto Rico.

In 1986, he joined the WWF (now WWE) as Haku and formed a tag team called The Islanders with Tama (The Tonga Kid). The Islanders won the 1986 Battle Royal in New York and won a six man tag team match at Wrestlemania IV.

One of Haku's greatest moments was the day he was able to send money to help his family back in Tonga. "See Mum and Dad, I'm getting somewhere," he said, "even though I'm not a doctor!"

In 1988, Tonga was crowned King of the WWF and took the name King Haku. He defended his crown against Harley Race at the 1989 Royal Rumble. He then formed a tag team called The Colossal Connection with Andre the Giant and they won the WWF Tag Team Championship.

Haku also fought for the individual world championship against The Ultimate Warrior. He lost the match but gave The Ultimate Warrior all he could handle. Haku left the WWF after competing in the 1992 Royal Rumble.

In 1994, he joined the WCW under the name Meng and formed a tag team called The Faces of Fear. His character was a former bodyguard of the Emperor of Japan and his finishing move was the Tongan Death Grip.

"If I had a gun and was sitting inside a tank with one shell left and Meng is 300 yards away … the first thing I'm going to do is jump out of the tank and shoot myself," said Hall of Fame wrestler, Jake "The Snake" Roberts.

Meng fought Goldberg for the WCW World Championship in 1998. In 2001, he won the WCW Hardcore Championship. He was the last WCW Hardcore champion.

Haku returned to the WWE for the 2001 Royal Rumble and retired soon after.

The WWE website says Haku was "perhaps the toughest man to step into a ring. The mention of his name sent a chill up the spine of his foes, and his friends too."

Tonga mentored many wrestlers during his career, including Dwayne 'The Rock' Johnson. When The Rock first auditioned for the WWF, he had no costume and no money. Who did he call for help? Uncle Tonga, that's who.

"Uncle Tonga is a humble man and a champion," The Rock says. "He's one of the greatest people I know. I'll never forget what he did for me when I had nothing."

Since 2003, Tonga has been in semi-retirement, although amazingly, he still wrestles from time to time in special promotions. In 2016, at the age of 56, he formed a tag team with Samoan-New Zealander, Liger, and won the New Zealand Tag Team Championship! NOTE: Liger is Michel Mulipola, the illustrator of this book!

"You might think wrestling is fake," Tonga says. "But to me it's a job. It's a way of providing for my family. And it helps me put Tonga on the map."

Tongan families will never forget the unique promos he did in the 1980s and 1990s, speaking in the Tongan language and raising awareness of his culture. "I love it when Tongans support their country and their sports teams," Tonga says.

Haku delivers the Tongan Death Kick to fellow wrestling legend Andre the Giant.

THE TCW – TONGAN CHAMPIONSHIP OF WRESTLING

William Anderson was a surgeon on Captain James Cook's ship which visited Tonga in 1777. He wrote down things he saw in a journal, including an ancient form of wrestling:

"They lay hold of each other, with a hand on each side, and he who succeeds in drawing his antagonist to him immediately tries to lift him and throw him upon his back … If they be equally matched, they endeavour to throw each other by entwining their legs, or lifting each other from the ground … When one is thrown he immediately quits the field; but the victor sits down for a few seconds, then gets up, and goes to the side he came from, who proclaim the victory aloud, in a sentence delivered slowly, and in a musical cadence. No person who has been vanquished can engage with his conqueror a second time i.e. no rematches … It also often happens, that five or six rise from each side, and challenge together."

"Being Tongan inspired me to be the best wrestler I could be. When you come from being poor and hungry, your only thought is to go after everything with a strong, warrior attitude because you want to make life better for your family.

"Your culture gives you strength because we come from tough lives. So go get it!"

HON. 'AKILISI POHIVA 

(1941-)
Politician

Village: Fakakai, Ha'apai

From the 1960s, a group of citizens emerged in Tonga who wanted more say in the running of the country than previous generations had. 'Akilisi Pohiva was one of those people.

'Akilisi studied History and Politics at the University of the South Pacific in Fiji. These subjects showed him that there were many different types of government in the world. Maybe one of them might work well in Tonga.

When 'Akilisi went home to Tonga, he taught at Tonga Teachers' College. He also joined the pro-democracy movement.

"The King had the ultimate power to rule the country," he said. "Our mission was to change that system to allow the people to participate directly in running our government."

In the early 1980s, 'Akilisi began a radio program that became popular in Tonga. The program often criticised the way the Tongan government was running the country. In 1985, the government dismissed him from the program.

But 'Akilisi wouldn't stay quiet about the things that concerned him. He started a newspaper, the *Koe Kele'a*, with some friends. Koe Kele'a looked deeply at issues important to Tongan society at the time.

The government struck back at 'Akilisi again – they fired him from his job at the teachers' college, with no explanation.

'Akilisi responded by taking the government to the Supreme Court for wrongful dismissal. The court decided that 'Akilisi was right. It was an important moment in Tongan history - the first time that a citizen had won a victory over the government in court.

'Akilisi's fight for justice inspired others. Another three people took the government to court for wrongful dismissal and won.

Sometimes the best way to change something is from the inside. 'Akilisi ran for parliament in 1987 and was elected as one of the people's representatives.

The people's representatives had many concerns: Why did some people in the government receive large pay increases while others got none? Why were Tongan passports sold to non-citizens? How come poor people paid more taxes than rich people?

But though they had a voice in parliament, the people's representatives were outnumbered by the nobles and ministers that the King chose. Whenever they asked for changes, they were outvoted.

'Akilisi and the people's representatives continued to ask for peaceful change. In 1988, they presented a 7000 signature petition to the King. None of their requests were granted.

Many people became angry and frustrated that life in Tonga wasn't changing as they hoped. In 2006, some workers went on strike because they wanted fairer wages. The strike ended in rioting which killed six people and destroyed many of the businesses in Nuku'alofa.

When George Tupou V became King in 2008, he promised to give up some of his royal powers. He said that from now on the Tongan government would be elected by the people. "I'm glad the King is doing the right thing," 'Akilisi said. "The war is nearly over."

In 2010, Siale 'Ataongo Kaho became Tonga's first Prime Minister not chosen by the monarch. The parliament was made up of nine nobles and 17 people's representatives. The people's representatives were now the majority, just as the King promised they would be.

'Akilisi Pohiva also formed a political party - the Democratic Party of the Friendly Islands. In the 2014 elections he was chosen as the second elected Prime Minister in Tongan history.

'Akilisi is recognised in the Pacific and internationally for his work in helping Tonga to become a democratic country. But it's come at a great cost, especially to his family. He's been jailed twice, persecuted by the government, attacked physically and called a traitor.

It's a cost 'Akilisi and others were willing to pay for the sake of their beloved Tonga.

TONGANS IN CHARGE

In 2008, Carmel Sepuloni became the first Tongan to serve in the New Zealand parliament. Carmel is of Tongan, Samoan and European descent. Jenny Lātū Salesa is a current Tongan MP in the New Zealand parliament. Achievement runs in Jenny's blood — many of her grandparents were *faifekau* (church ministers) and her father, Sāmiuela, was Tonga's first pharmacist. In 2011, Dr 'Ana Taufe'ulungaki became the first female Minister of Education in Tonga.

'Akilisi representing Tonga at the Annual
Defender of Democracy Awards Dinner,
Colombia 2013.

Kavaonau was a girl who lived in 'Eu'eiki with her mother, Fefafa and father, Fevanga. She was a very sick girl and some say her skin was covered in patchy white spots.

When Kavaonau died, she was buried in a grave near her home. A chief named Lo'au told her parents to look after the grave because something good would come from it.

Every day, Fevanga tended the grave and sat next to it talking to his beloved daughter.

After a while two plants grew out of the grave. One grew from Kavaonau's feet and the other grew from where her head was resting.

One morning, a rat scuttled by and Fevanga watched it stop to nibble on the plant that grew from Kavaonau's head.

After eating, the rat appeared to stumble as if it was drunk. It fell down near the plant at Kavaonau's feet and began nibbling on that one too. The second plant seemed to revive the rat.

Fevanga took the plants to Lo'au and told him what he had seen.

"We will name the plant Kava, in memory of your daughter," Lo'au said.

Lo'au told his servants to bring a wooden bowl, some fau fibre and a cup. With these implements he made the first kava drink.

Some people believe there are other connections between Kavaonau and kava. They say the segments of the trunk are her intestines and that those who drink too much kava develop leprous skin like Kavaonau's.

Lo'au delivered the kava root to the Tu'i Tonga who formed the first kava circle. The kava circle and the ceremonies connected with it are important because they reflect the status system of Tonga.

In some stories Lo'au is a chief from Ha'amea, Tongatapu. He lived during the reign of Momo, the tenth Tu'i Tonga. Others say that he was a foreigner, possibly from Samoa or Tahiti.

Kava became an important part of life in Tonga. It is used in formal ceremonies as well as by commoners.

Before fishermen in 'Eue'iki go out to catch sharks they hold a kava ceremony. The first cup is thrown into the sea as an offering for Hina.

One of the interesting ways kava is used is in courtship rituals.

If a young man wants to meet a girl he can ask a close friend to organise a kava ceremony with her family and friends. The friend in this situation is called the Moa Uli (Black Fowl). It's the Moa Uli's job to keep everyone entertained at the kava ceremony so the couple have time to talk.

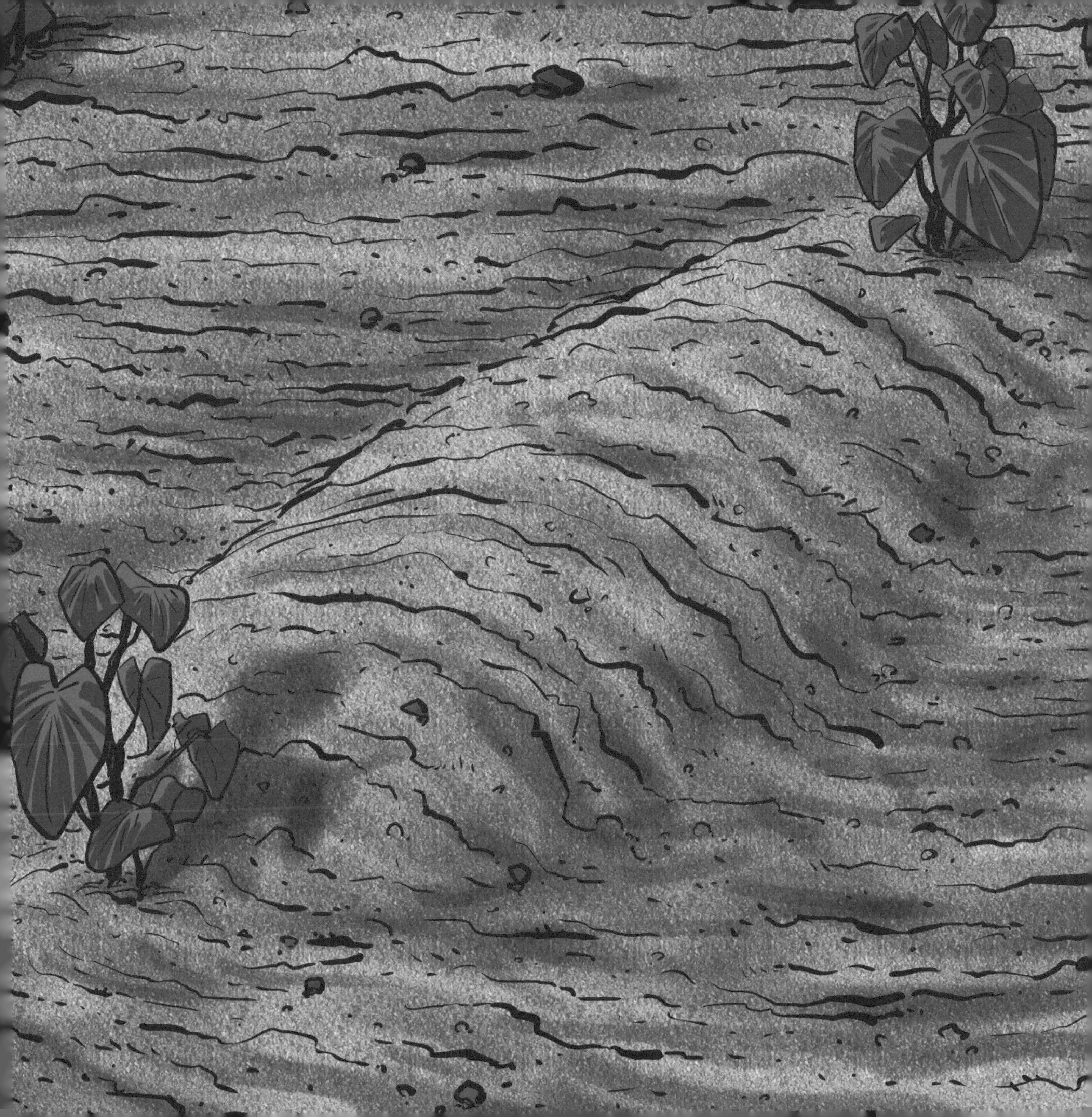

In many western countries, Tongan youth are encouraged to attend kalapu kava (kava clubs) as an alternative to going to nightclubs and pubs. Kalapu kava are a way for Tongan young people to learn about their culture and traditions in a safe environment.

Tongans also give kava as gifts to visitors.

When the first Europeans arrived in their ships, villagers rowed out to meet them and the first thing they did was offer kava, sometimes throwing the kava roots on board the ship.

A Dutch expedition in the year 1616 rejected the kava gifts because they thought the Tongans were trying to poison them!

Captain James Cook had a different view of the gift.

"One could not wish for a better sign of friendship than this," he said when offered kava. "Can we make a friend feel more welcome than by setting before him the best liquor that we have got? In this manner did these friendly people receive us."

No wonder Cook named Tonga the Friendly Islands!

LETTER TO FEIFAFA

Legends say that Kava'onau, the daughter of Feifafa and Fevanga, was sacrificed so the visiting King would have something to eat. Tongan poet Dr Konai Helu Thaman, wrote a poem inspired by this story - a message of sympathy for a mother who has lost her daughter.

tear-stained tapa

soaked in blood

continue to flow

from the over-filled kava bowl

of our rulers

their quick acceptance

of your sacrifice

still bleeds

at the cutting edge

of time

i have been thinking

over what you did

that dark day long ago

i still don't believe

that a king was worth it!

(Letter to Feifafa)

SISTER MALIA TUIFU'A

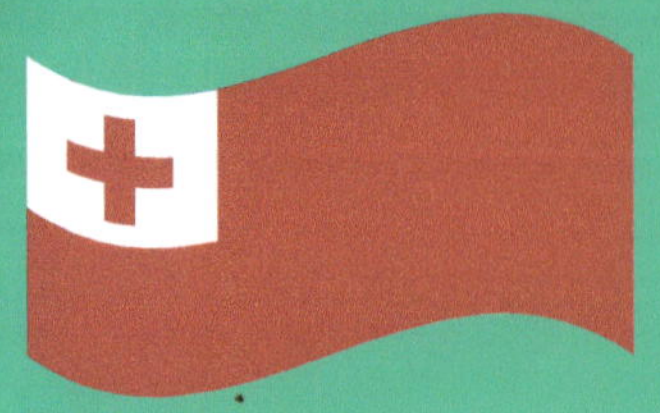

(1924-2007)
Community worker

Village: Lapaha

Sister Malia Tuifu'a's life mission was helping poor people in Tonga. She especially wanted to improve the lives of Tongan women and she gained international recognition for her work.

Malia was born a twin. When she was delivered doctors feared something might be wrong because she wasn't moving. But when heated nonu leaves were pressed on to her body, she screamed, and her family cheered - God had special plans for this little warrior.

Her father named her, Malia Tupou Falemei. The family asked Queen Salote to name the twins as well because they were related to her. Salote gave Malia the name, Halakihe'umata (Road to the Rainbow).

Because their mother was Catholic, the twins attended Catholic schools during their childhood. Their first school was St.Therese's Convent in Lapaha which was run by French nuns.

Malia was a clever student and enjoyed English, Tongan, maths and geography. Later in life Malia admitted she was a naughty child, both at school and at home. She often neglected to do her chores and was sometimes cheeky to elders. On one occasion, Malia and some friends were strapped at school for misbehaving. The "strap" the teacher used was a stingray's tail!

One thing Malia especially loved was performing in kātoanga 'ofa (fundraising events) for the Catholic church. Many of the lakalaka she danced in were composed by Queen Salote.

In 1946, Malia travelled on a boat to Vava'u to attend a funeral. The sea was rough and the boat rocked from side to side so violently that Malia thought it was going to overturn. "Dear Lord Jesus," she prayed. "If you keep me alive, I will dedicate my life to serving you."

Malia and other sisters on Profession Day, 1950.

The boat arrived safely at Vava'u and Malia went straight to the Convent and told the Mother Superior about her promise. Mother Superior explained what becoming a sister in the Catholic church would mean – a life devoted to prayer and service of the poor, sick and uneducated. They prayed together that God would guide Malia's decision.

At first Malia's father didn't want her to become a Catholic sister, but her mother encouraged her to follow her heart and eventually her father supported her too.

In 1950, Malia celebrated Profession Day – the day she officially gave her life to God and the Catholic church - "fua kava ki ke mate" (until the day I die). She chose Sister Augustino as her new name, after the legendary Saint Augustine. Malia admired Augustine's humility and strength to overcome challenges in his life.

Sisters were later given permission to use a family name and Malia took the name her father gave her. She became Sister Malia Tuifu'a.

Malia was a skilled teacher and taught in primary schools all over Tonga. But the work she loved most of all was helping Tongan women to have happier lives, especially the poor and forgotten.

Tongan women faced many challenges at this time, including lack of money for clothing, food and school fees; health issues; and domestic abuse.

One of Malia's first projects was kautaha (work groups). She encouraged women to help each other use their artistic skills to make mats and ngatu for weddings and funerals and handcrafts to sell in markets. That way they could earn extra income for their families and wouldn't have to rely on family overseas or have to borrow money.

She raised funds nationally and internationally to build houses, concrete water tanks, and clean water facilities for needy families. She also raised money to build community halls and repair damaged homes after cyclones.

Many international organisations supported Malia's work with the poorest of the poor in Tonga. She was invited to speak to conferences all over the world about her work.

Sister Malia's motto was: "Happy mothers make happy families, happy families make happy villages, and happy villages make for a happy country."

Thanks to Sister Malia and others like her, the lives of Tongan women became happier and healthier.

HEALTH BY THE PEOPLE FOR THE PEOPLE

'Eseta Fifita Finau is another Tongan achiever with great love for the community. 'Eseta is the President of the Tongan Nurses Association of New Zealand. She grew up in Tonga, went to Tonga High School and studied nursing in Sydney, Australia. "I wanted to do something that would make a difference to the lives of our people," she says. 'Eseta believes Tongan nurses play a very important role in the community. "Sometimes a patient would go and see a palangi doctor and say things like, 'I've got this cold feeling. I can feel death coming up my leg.' The palangi doctor would refer them to the psychiatrist because they thought they were nutty. But it was a Tongan term to describe a feeling … the sort of statement that would only be understood by a Tongan."

JOHN TUI

Villages: Talafo'ou, Ha'asini, Ma'ufanga, Hofoa

John Tui is a trailblazing Tongan actor who has performed alongside some of the most famous entertainers in the world. He's been performing his whole life – dancing with his sisters in Tongan cultural events; acting and singing in school productions; and making a living in professional film and theatre.

John's parents emigrated from Tonga in the 1970s and raised their family of nine children in Manurewa, South Auckland. John is the oldest child and his parents taught him early on that he was to be a role model for the younger ones.

John's life path was set when he was made the lead character in a school production of Solomon. "I absolutely loved it," he says. "And that's when I knew that acting was my calling."

John's parents didn't agree with his "calling" at first. "They didn't mind me acting as a hobby but they tried to guide me away from it as a career," he says. "They were migrants and they hoped I'd be a doctor or a lawyer or a stable occupation like that."

But you just couldn't get John off the stage! Though he played rugby for James Cook High School - acting was his first love. "It was unheard of to see one of the boys acting," John laughs. "But my friends respected it because they saw it gave me a more open minded view of the world."

After school, John worked for a little while in menial jobs that he hated. "Those jobs made my heart bleed," he says. "My parents came here for me to do more than work in a factory for someone else. I knew I had to do something better with my life."

At the age of 26, with his wife's encouragement, John left his job and enrolled in Drama at the Unitec School of Performing Arts.

His first big acting opportunity was a lead role in Disney's Power Rangers. He was possibly the first Tongan to perform in a production as large as that.

On the set of Disney's Power Rangers.

One of John's favourite moments was bringing his parents on set.

"I wanted them to see that I was doing well so they'd be proud of me," he says. "I think that's the moment they finally accepted this career choice I had made."

John's experience grew as he performed in a number of New Zealand films, plays and television programs. Some of these included Outrageous Fortune, Go Girls and Shortland Street.

It's difficult to find regular work as an actor in New Zealand and sometimes John had to take jobs like painting, building and even babysitting to help support his family of four children.

Meanwhile, producers of a new Hollywood film called Battleship had a problem. Despite two years of searching, they couldn't find an actor suitable to play Navy Lieutenant 'The Beast' Lynch. They opened auditions for actors in New Zealand and Australia and John won the role.

Before flying to Hawaii to begin filming, he spent some time looking at photos in old family albums. He wanted the images to burn into his soul so he would always remember where he came from.

John says he was a little nervous on his first day on set because he was going to be working with Liam Neeson, one of his favourite actors. He didn't have to worry. "He had a really humble attitude," John says. "And it was so good to see that someone of his stature wasn't affected by the fame. He carried himself with real humility."

Rhianna was another world famous performer in the film and John was amazed at how much attention was paid to her. "To see fifty paparazzi cars chasing her everywhere was shocking to me," he says. "She was only twenty two then and handled it really well. She reminded me of my sisters, young and gifted."

Though working with some of the most well-known entertainers in the world, John wasn't star struck at all. "They're just ordinary people who love performing like I do," he says. "They're your work colleagues and you've got a job to do."

With Rihanna at the Sydney premiere of Battleship.

The most challenging thing for John was being away from his family. Hollywood has many temptations and he was determined not to fall. He even convinced the film's producers to fly his family over to be with him.

To perform in a Hollywood big budget film is a major goal for most actors. Some people change when they reach that level of success. Not John. When he came back to New Zealand, he deliberately wore jandals and shorts through Customs. "I wanted everyone to know that I hadn't changed, I was still me," he says.

Then he bought both sets of parents a home. "That's the island way. It's all about looking after our families."

The list of John's credits continues to grow. In 2015, he starred in the New Zealand film, Born To Dance and played the Orc commander in The Hobbit: The Battle of the Five Armies.

"I've always been passionate about acting, whether it's Shakespeare, TV or film," he says. "To be the first major Tongan actor makes my parents, family and friends proud, as it does me being a Polynesian from the South Pacific."

"My Tongan heritage is very important to me. Being able to speak and understand Tongan gives me a close connection with Tonga and a deeper understanding of myself, my family and how we value women and elders."

No matter where John's acting takes him you can be sure he will always remember who he is and where he comes from. This is a message he has for young people as well. "Accept yourself and love who you are," he says. "Try to be the best version of yourself that you can and don't worry about being someone else."

"Be honest with what you truly want to do. If you're passionate then it will be easier to go through the hard times that will definitely come."

TONGAN BROTHERS ON THE RISE

Tongan-Samoan-European brothers, Joe and Rene Naufahu are actors, businessmen, filmmakers and two of the most successful and inspiring Tongan achievers. Their home village is Kolonga, on the island of Tongatapu.

Rene was one of the first Polynesian actors to appear on New Zealand television when he played Sam Aleni on Shortland Street. He's acted in films like The Matrix Revolutions (2003) and Power Rangers Samurai (2011). Rene is also a writer (The Market) and director (The Last Saint).

Joe Naufahu is one of the most prominent Tongan actors working at the moment. He's appeared in a number of popular TV shows including Go Girls, Spartacus and Game of Thrones.

Joe is also the Founder of the Ludus Magnus fitness centres. "If you want to achieve your dreams in life, then be prepared for failure and rejection because it is inevitable," Joe says. "If you aren't prepared for it and you don't learn from it then it will be useless to you."

In ancient Tonga, Pulotu was an island paradise where the spirits of chiefs went when they died. It was also the home of Hikule'o, the sister of Tangaloa and Maui and one of the most powerful beings in the Tongan universe.

Four men with supernatural powers didn't want to wait until they died to see Pulotu - they decided to go and see it while they were still alive. Their names were Haveatoke (Slippery Eel), Fakafūmaka (Big Rock), Haelefeke (Walking Octopus) and Lohi.

A woman named Faimalie (Great Performer) asked them to take her as well.

"There's not enough room in the canoe," one of the men said. "And anyway, what use do we have of a woman?"

"I'll sit on the outrigger part of the canoe so I won't take up any room," she pleaded. "You won't be sorry."

The five adventurers reached Pulotu and nervously dragged their canoe up on the beach. Just then, they saw movement coming from Hikule'o's fale. Fakafūmaka pretended to be a rock and sat perfectly still. Lohi transformed into an insect and crawled on to Hikule'o's roof. The other three buried themselves in the ground.

"I know intruders are here," Hikule'o said to her guards. "Look, there's a foreign canoe. Find the trespassers and bring them to me."

But the strangers were so well hidden and disguised that the guards were unable to find them.

"Fools!" Hikule'o spat. "I need to bring out my experts. Skilful Eyes, Smart Ears, Stunning Nose … I know you guys can find them with your sensory powers."

But Hikule'o's sensory experts also failed to find the intruders.

"Okay you strangers, you're too clever for my guards and experts," Hikule'o called. "Come out now so we can talk."

The five Tongan heroes emerged from their hiding places and cautiously approached Hikule'o.

"I don't know why you're smiling," she continued. "Do you really think that you people are superior to us? We will now hold a kava ceremony. And you must finish every drop of the kava … or you die."

"Too easy!" the strangers laughed, but their confidence evaporated when they saw one hundred of Hikule'o's servants carrying twenty kava roots, each the size of a coconut tree trunk. When the kava was prepared it filled a bowl the size of a lagoon.

The four males of the group began to scoop up cups of the muddy brown liquid. But they underestimated the strength of the kava. After just three cups each they began to stumble senselessly into each other. "There's nooooooo way!" they cried and began weeping.

"Remember when you questioned the use of a woman?" Faimalie said. Then she climbed into the kava bowl and

began to wade through it taking huge gulps. When the kava was all gone, she ate the bowl, the strainers, the stalks and the twenty coconut trees. Talk about a big appetite!

"Well done Faimalie," Hikule'o said. "Men always underestimate women."

Hikule'o raised her arm and her cooks brought out an enormous spit-roasted pig, a thirty foot long feke boiled in coconut cream, fifty bowls of lu ika and fifteen baskets of 'umu-cooked breadfruit, taro and yams. The food was stacked so high that it blocked out the sun.

"Eat all of it … or you die," Hikule'o ordered.

The four men had never seen food like this before and they were so hungry they attacked the feast like hungry sharks. But the food was richer than anything they had ever tasted and soon they were writhing on the ground in pain, rubbing their over-full stomachs.

Once again, Faimalie came to the rescue. Not only did she eat the mountain of food, but she ate the leaves the food was wrapped in, the mats, the baskets and the hot cooking stones as well.

Hikule'o began to get angry. There was no way these strangers were going to get the better of her.

"Now we're going to have a surfing contest," she said. "Choose someone to compete against my best surfer … but it can't be Faimalie."

Slippery Eel was inspired by Faimalie and stepped forward. The contest was close. In the first two races, the surfers rode all the way into shore with neither falling off. In the third race, they disappeared into the barrel of a massive wave. When they were hidden from view, Slippery Eel bit the neck of his opponent, killing him instantly. He rode into shore on his own while his opponent's body washed up on the beach.

"I see that your men are skilful after all," Hikule'o said. "One more challenge to prove who is the greatest between my people and yours: a diving contest. Whoever can stay under the water the longest, wins."

Big Rock stepped forward. He and his opponent went out to the deepest part of the ocean, jumped in and sank to the bottom. Minutes, hours, days and weeks passed and the two men sat firmly on the sea floor, staring into each other's eyes. Finally, after a month Big Rock's opponent's eyes began to bulge and his cheeks turned purple. He thrust himself upwards to the surface. Big Rock was the winner.

"Okay okay I get it, you're all really good at what you do," Hikule'o said exasperated. "This is it though. I promise this is definitely the last challenge to prove once and for all who is the greatest: you or us."

"This is something you can never do. See that vi tree?" She pointed to a tree that was so wide it would take a day to walk around and stretched so far into the sky that its fruit looked like stars. "Pick all the fruit. If you drop even one … you die."

Walking Octopus stepped forward winking. "I got this guys," he said. He lay on his back and lifted his legs into the air. Magically his legs transformed into tentacles. He carefully plucked each piece of fruit from the tree and gently placed them all in a basket.

"Now eat them all," Hikule'o commanded.

Faimalie sprang to her feet and began gobbling the fruit. "Noooooo, I forgot to say, not Faimalie!" Hikule'o cried.

"Too late!" Faimalie laughed, devouring the fruit in huge handfuls. When she finished she ate all the leaves off the tree and the branches and the trunk too.

"Okay that's it you win, go back to your own land before you leave us with nothing!" Hikule'o screamed.

The five Tongan heroes reclined in their canoe grinning at each other as they sailed back to Tonga.

"I told you that you wouldn't be sorry for taking me along," Faimalie said.

"You're right sis," the men agreed.

"But that's not all," she said, revealing a little bag she had kept concealed. "I had to take a little something before we left."

Faimalie opened the bag and a small clump of taro roots fell on to the deck of the canoe. Her four companions laughed as they too revealed hidden breadfruit and yam roots to take home for the people of Tonga.

HON. BARON VAEA

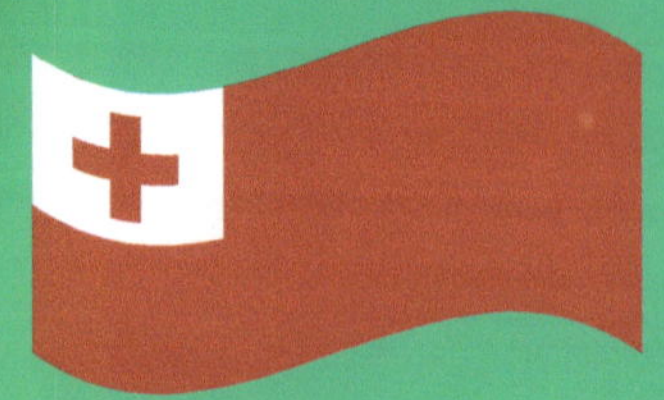

(1921-2009)
Pilot / Politician

Village: Houma

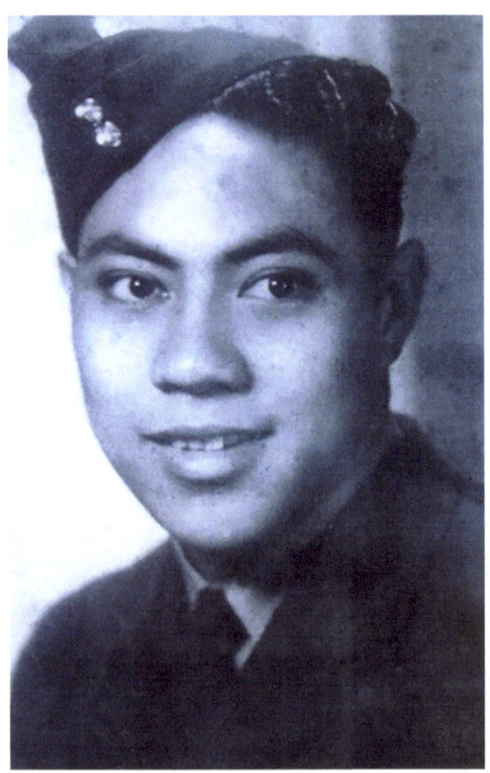

Baron Vaea was the first Pacific Islander to fly in the Royal New Zealand Air Force. He was a pioneer who lived through the reign of three monarchs and served the Tongan government for fifty four years.

Baron Vaea was born 'Alipate Halakilangi Tupou. He was a grandson of King George Tupou II and a nephew of Queen Salote. As a young man he attended Tupou College.

The children of titled families were expected to do some of their schooling overseas and 'Alipate's family organised for him to go to Wesley College in Auckland. 'Alipate was reluctant to leave his beloved Tonga, but he had no choice. "If you stay here you won't know anything about the world, so you must go," his parents said.

World War Two broke out while 'Alipate was in New Zealand and he joined the New Zealand Army. Later, he transferred to the Royal New Zealand Air Force and became the first Tongan pilot to be commissioned.

'Alipate was excited about learning to fly planes. "Coming from the islands, flying was something new," he said, "and it just settled in my mind." He read as much as he could about some of the legendary fighter pilots of World War One.

He dreamed of flying Spitfires in Europe like his heroes did. But the RNZAF had a more important role for him. He trained to fly in small Tiger Moths and Harvards and when he had mastered those planes, he moved on to larger Catalinas.

"Catalinas are challenging," he said. "You have to manoeuvre them like a ship because you're thinking of the wind."

After 'Alipate completed his training, he was called to serve in the Pacific. He was given many interesting missions including patrolling for submarines; carrying out search and rescues; and flying supplies to war zones. 'Alipate served from 1942 to 1945.

Graduation photo to celebrate the end of pilot training with the RNZAF.

Though he was the only Pacific Island pilot in the RNZAF, he always felt valued. "I was accepted just the same as everybody else," he said. "I was very proud to be in the Air Force and my people in Tonga were also very proud of me."

At the end of the war, 'Alipate returned to Tonga and was appointed to the prestigious Vaea title.

Vaea held many leadership positions during his life. He was an agricultural inspector for Queen Salote and then Governor of Ha'apai from 1960 to 1968. At different times he served the Tongan people in government as minister of agriculture, commerce, education, fisheries and forestry, industries, labour and tourism.

In 1969, Vaea was appointed Tonga's first High Commissioner to the United Kingdom and was given the title, Baron Vaea.

Baron Vaea was determined to ensure that Tonga had a strong presence in the Pacific. He attended the first regional leaders' meeting and spoke passionately about the need for Pacific unity.

His experiences in World War Two had shown him what a tragic thing war is. He stressed the importance of communication to resolve disputes.

In 1991, he became the 12th Prime Minister of Tonga. One of his main concerns was helping the youth of Tonga. He wanted to give them more opportunities and initiated many special youth training programs.

"Sometimes I think it would be best if Tonga changes for the benefit of our young people," he said. "We should let go of some of our beliefs and the way we do things that seem to weigh us down."

Baron Vaea retired in 2000 at the age of 78. He left a tremendous legacy as one of the longest serving civil servants in Tongan history, a Methodist preacher, storyteller, performer of traditional dance, composer, orator ... and World War Two pilot!

FAMILI TIES

The current Queen of Tonga, Her Majesty Queen Nanasipau'u Tuku'aho, is the daughter of Baron Vaea.

MANU VATUVEI

(1986-)
Rugby League player

Villages: Ha'afeva, Tataka mo Tonga

Manu Vatuvei is one of the most successful Tongan rugby league players in history.

Manu grew up in Otara, South Auckland, the second youngest of five children. He played rugby league for the Otara Scorpions and Otahuhu Leopards as a child. His favourite league player was fellow Tongan, Gorden Tallis.

Coaches liked to put Manu on the wing because he was quick. But he was also usually the biggest player on the field and junior opponents couldn't believe he was the same age as them. They were right. He was a year younger!

Manu says he was tempted to use alcohol and drugs and to join gangs when he was growing up. He thought they were cool. That changed when his older brother went to jail.

"This is what gang life is really like," his brother told him one day during a prison visit. "There's nothing cool about this."

Manu decided that he no longer wanted to be a gangster, he wanted to be successful. His way to do that was through the game of rugby league.

When he was 16, Manu joined the New Zealand Warriors development squad.

"It was a huge achievement for not only me but my family as well," Manu said. "I looked at my Dad's face and he was really happy and that made me hungry to achieve more."

Manu played his first NRL game for the Warriors on 23 May, 2004 against the South Sydney Rabbitohs. Though he was just 18 years old, he stood 1.89 metres tall, weighed 112 kilograms and had the wildest blonde afro ever seen on a rugby league field!

"The most intimidating player in rugby league."

If the Warriors needed a winger to worry opposition with his sheer speed, Manu could do that. If they needed a winger to trample over the top of would-be tacklers, he could do that. And if they needed a winger to leap acrobatically and plant the ball on the try line with one hand while the rest of his body floated sideways in the air, Manu could do that too!

Manu was once named the most intimidating player in league, making him a major target for defenders. He didn't mind.

"I like being a target," he says. "I've been dazed sometimes but I try not to show it. I try to act tough. It motivates me to run even harder."

Rugby league is a physical sport and Manu's had lots of injuries during his career. "I feel like I always have a knee injury," he says. "I'll definitely have knee problems when I retire. I'll probably be on crutches or in a wheelchair."

In 2007, Manu faced a major challenge - he dropped the ball six times in a game against the Parramatta Eels. Three of the drops led to tries and the Warriors lost the game. "He's a clumsy klutz," said one commentator. "He's got hands like a dolphin's flippers," said another.

"There's a lot of obstacles that you'll go through in your career and that was a big one for myself," Manu said.

In 2008, the Warriors went back to Parramatta and some people thought Manu might struggle again. They were wrong. Manu scored three tries to help the Warriors beat the Eels. "That was my Redemption Day!" he said. "Hopefully I showed that if I can get through it, everyone else can."

Another challenge has been coping with the loss of loved ones. Every time he scores a try, Manu honours his late grandparents and close friend Sonny Fai, by pointing to the sky.

In 2016, Manu went through one of his hardest times as a player, struggling with harsh comments people made about him and his team on Facebook and Twitter.

"I try to hide things with my laugh but it does hurt," he says. "And when people say things about me it doesn't just hurt me, it hurts my family too.

"It's the toughest thing when my kids come home crying because of things people are saying and I want to protect them from that."

A big reason why Manu is able to overcome these obstacles is his faith in God. Before each game he writes his family name on the strapping of one wrist and his favourite Bible verse on the other: "I can do all things through Christ who strengthens me."

Then he prays

Manu also finds inspiration from other people. One of those who inspired him the most was All Black legend, Jonah Lomu. "Not many people knew what Jonah was going through," Manu says. "But just knowing that and seeing what he achieved, how he kept going no matter what obstacles were put in front of him – that inspires me."

One of Manu's happiest moments was the day he bought a home for his parents and siblings. "My first goal when I started playing was to buy my parents a house," he said. "I've ticked that now."

That loving nature is a big reason why Warriors fans and teammates love Manu and why he's one of the most popular players in league. Some fans even offered to contribute to his contract because they never want him to leave the Warriors!

"He's the most giving player that I have ever coached," said former coach Matt Elliott.

Tongan culture plays a big part in everything Manu does. He speaks and understands Tongan. He proudly wears his famous nifo koula (gold teeth) which he received from an auntie's gold ring to commemorate his first trip to Tonga. He even played the trombone in his church brass band.

"Sometimes I wish I grew up in Tonga so I could understand how they do things over there," Manu says. "Then I could probably speak the language better."

"My parents were strict about us speaking Tongan at home and I used to think I was good at speaking Tongan. But when I hear guys from Tonga like Solomone Kata speaking, it puts me off a little!"

Manu is actively involved in community work and encourages children and young people to stay away from negative influences and to aim to be successful people.

"I know how hard it is growing up," he says. "Sometimes you don't have everything that other people have. But make the most of school.

"Don't leave school with regrets because when you grow up you realise what you've done and you can't take anything back."

"Never give up," Manu continues. "There'll be lots of obstacles and it's never easy, but if you have the mentality of never giving up and if you focus, you can achieve your goals."

TURN IT INTO SOMETHING GOOD

Everyone fails sometimes, and that's okay ... it doesn't mean you can't be successful.

The man who dropped the ball six times in one game went on to become one of the best rugby league players in the world:

- Most tries in Warriors history
- Most tries in Kiwi history
- First player in rugby league history to score 10+ tries in ten straight seasons
- International Winger of the Year and World Champion in 2008
- Voted the NRL's Favourite Son in 2014
- NRL All Stars (2010, 2012, 2015)

RUGBY LEAGUE WEEK
AUSTRALIA'S NO.1 LEAGUE MAGAZINE
MARCH 24, 2010 $5.70 (incl. GST) NZ $6.00 (incl.GST)
WIN! $500 BSC PACK
THE BEAST
Is this the most feared man in the NRL?
FARAH SHOCK
WHY I ALMOST QUIT THE TIGERS
FEELING COCKY
ROOSTERS WARN: BEST IS YET TO COME
BIRD FURY
DON'T HANG OFFENDERS OUT TO DRY
RIDING HIGH
WILLIE MANIA TAKES HOLD IN TOWNSVILLE
BONUS POSTER
Print post approved PP25500300543
9 313006 001805

NO MEAN FEET

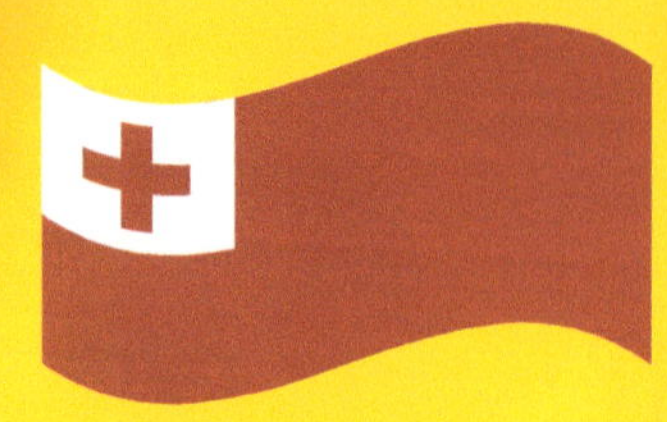

One morning in ancient Tonga, a man went out gardening while his pregnant wife rested at home. That same day, the woman gave birth to a son who she named Malie.

The woman was overjoyed and loved Malie, but when she looked at his little feet, she saw that they were deformed.

She didn't want her husband to see the baby's misshapen feet, so she abandoned him in a nearby forest.

The woman didn't know that a tevolo (demon) also lived in the forest. He was out hunting for food when he found the child. He took him home planning to eat him for dinner.

That evening, the tevolo was just about to eat the boy when he noticed its crooked feet.

"Eeeuuuw!" he said "They don't look nice to eat. Anyway this child is too small. I'll wait until he grows bigger so there's more of him to eat!"

He placed the boy in the loft of his fale and looked after him as he grew.

Meanwhile the woman gave birth to another child with deformed feet. Like the first one she was ashamed of him and abandoned him in the forest. The tevolo found the child and took him home too.

This happened eight more times which meant the tevolo now had ten children living in his loft, all growing there until they were big enough to eat.

Every morning the tevolo stood under the loft and instructed the children to poke their legs through a small hole so that he could see if their feet had grown straight.

As the children grew older their deformities disappeared and their feet grew normally.

Only Malie still had deformed feet.

"Oh what, your feet are still crooked and nasty!" the tevolo complained when Malie poked his feet through the hole.
"When are you ever going to grow out of that? Next one."

"He's going to see that my feet are normal now and he's going to eat me," cried the second born to his brothers.

"No he won't," said Malie and poked his own feet through again.

He did this eight more times and tricked the tevolo into thinking all the children still had deformed feet.

"What kind of family are you!" moaned the tevolo and stormed outside to go hunting.

"I've had enough of being imprisoned in this loft, waiting for the day he catches us out," said Malie. "Today's the day we leave."

The ten siblings jumped down from the loft and ran into the forest.

After running a little while, nine of the brothers realised that one person was struggling to keep up with them – it was their older brother, Malie, whose feet were still deformed.

"Keep going, I'll be okay," he called when he saw them stop.

"We'll never leave one of our brothers behind," they replied and slowed down so that he could keep up with them.

When the tevolo came home from hunting, he knew that someone had been in his fale. He called up to the loft but there was no answer.

"Maybe they're asleep," he thought. But when he climbed into the loft to check, he saw only their empty sleeping mats. "They've tricked me!" he cried leaping down from the loft.

The tevolo had a strong sense of smell and he picked up a scent heading towards the village at the far end of the forest.

"Tuputupulefanua!" he called to the heavens. "Give them food!"

At that very moment a basket of hot taro and a roasted pig appeared miraculously in front of the exhausted and hungry siblings.

"Maybe the rulers of the forest feel sorry for us and have blessed us," one of them said. "Can we rest and eat?"

"I'm not sure about this," said Malie. "If something seems too good to be true, it usually is. Let's just grab a piece of food and keep it moving."

Deep in the forest, the tevolo's senses told him that his plan had failed.

"Tuputupulefanua!" he called again. "Place an obstacle in their path."

Immediately a wall of jagged volcanic rocks materialised in front of the brothers, blocking the trail. All the brothers were able to climb over the wall except Malie - his crooked feet could find no grip on the craggy rocks.

"Carry on, I'll be okay," he told them. "Even if you help me over, tevolo will think of new ways to stop us and eventually he will win. I have to end this once and for all. And it's these feet that will help me do it."

The brothers did as Malie asked and left him at the base of the wall. They didn't leave him completely alone though – they hid in a clump of trees just around the corner. If their older sibling needed them, they'd be there for him just like they promised.

The tevolo arrived at the wall, breathless and cursing. As the tevolo climbed over the wall, Malie lay on his back and wedged his disjointed feet into the spaces between the rocks. They fit perfectly. Then he shook the wall with all the power in his legs.

The wall began to crumble underneath the tevolo and he lost his balance and tumbled to the ground. Cracked pieces of rugged island rock fell on him, killing him instantly.

The happy brothers emerged from the forest shouting for joy and lifted Malie high in the air.

Never again would they be troubled by the tevolo and they promised to look after each other for the rest of their lives.

THE JETS

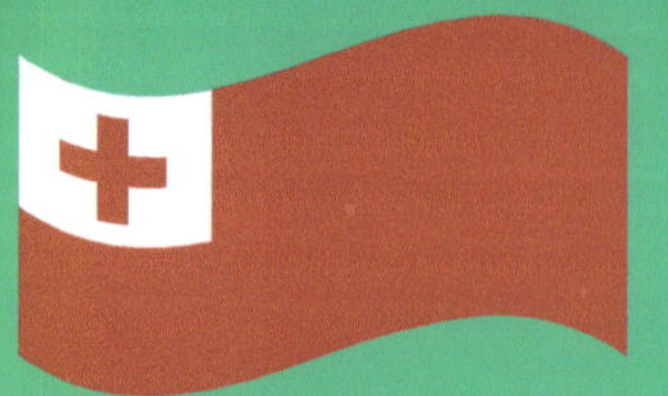

Musicians

Villages: Ha'aloufuli / Matahau

The Jets are a legendary Tongan musical group who had a number of popular hit singles in the late 1980s. They have eight Billboard top ten hits, three World Tours and a Grammy Award nomination to their name.

In 1965, Maikeli and Vake Wolfgramm left their home in Tonga and migrated to the United States in search of a better life. Their dreams would be fulfilled in a way they could only have imagined.

Maikeli and Vake settled in Minneapolis and raised a family of fifteen children. One thing that always brought the family together was music and they sang together at home, at church and at school.

In 1983, six of the Wolfgramm siblings signed a record deal with MCA Records. Two Samoan friends joined the group and they called themselves The Jets, after the song "Benny and the Jets", by Elton John. The original members were Leroy, Haini, Rudy, Kathi, Elizabeth and Moana Wolfgramm, along with Eugene Hunt and Eddie Lavatai.

The Jets' musical style reflected their upbringing as Polynesians living in a multicultural country. It was a mix of dance, Latin, pop and R&B music ... with a Pacific flavour.

It didn't take long for success to come their way. In 1986, their song "Crush On You" reached number three on the USA Billboard Hot 100.

Then came the number ones: "You Got It All" and "Make It Real" made it to the top of the Billboard adult contemporary chart. These slow jams are two of The Jets' most loved songs and are still heard on the radio today.

There were very few Polynesian artists performing at an international level at this time and The Jets helped raise awareness of Tongan artists and music in popular culture. They also did commercial endorsements with Doritos, Kool Aid, and Campbell's Soup.

The Jets – reunited and performing
all the hits they made famous.

But they weren't finished. In 1988, they had another hit song with "Sendin' All My Love" which reached number one on the Billboard dance charts.

Also in 1988, the group received a Grammy Award nomination for Best R&B Performance by a Group for "Rocket 2 U". A Grammy is the highest award possible in American music and only the most successful songs receive nominations.

The Jets' music was so popular, it featured on a number of blockbuster movie soundtracks including Beverly Hills Cop II ("Cross My Broken Heart"), Karate Kid III ("Under Any Moon"), Jaws The Revenge ("You Got It All") and Switch ("Sendin' Out A Message").

The Jets also sang at some of the world's most popular sporting events: the 1987 Baseball World Series, the 1988 Olympics, the 1991 Stanley Cup Finals, the 2002 Winter Olympics … only the very best groups in the world are invited to perform at such occasions.

One of the family's biggest highlights was a trip to Tonga in 1989 to perform for their people and King. "It was inspiring to see where our roots are," says Moana. "And getting on Tonga's postage stamp will always be a high honour as well."

Success often comes with challenges, and that was true for The Jets too. It wasn't easy to be so young and have to work in the stressful American music industry, especially with family members. In the early 90s the group decided to take a break.

But The Jets are a family as well as a group of entertainers. Their love for each other and for music brought them back together in 2010 to perform an anniversary concert in their hometown of Minneapolis, Minnesota. It felt good to perform together again and they wanted more. When it comes to family, it's always good to forgive and forget past hurts.

In 2013, most of The Jets reformed and released an album titled Reunited. The album features remakes of many of their hits along with new tracks.

In 2015-16, the group began touring again throughout the United States, reconnecting with fans who have supported them for over thirty years … and discovering a whole new generation of fans who love The Jets' music just as much as their parents do.

It's just one more reason why The Jets are regarded as one of the most loved and successful Polynesian bands in the history of music.

IN HARMONY WITH DINAH JANE HANSEN

Dinah is another Tongan singer making a name in the world of music. Dinah came to fame as a member of Fifth Harmony which finished third in the second season of X Factor America. Check out some of the awards Dinah and the group have won:

- Best US Act - 2015 MTV Europe Awards

- Favourite New Artist – 2015 Nickelodeon Kids' Choice Awards

- Favourite Group – 2016 People's Choice Awards

Music is in Dinah's blood – her brothers sang at church and her mum sang in a reggae band. From the age of eleven, Dinah's goal was to be a singer too. "The first time I performed I remember feeling so nervous and scared," Dinah says. "All I could think was, 'I hope they like me, I hope they don't boo.' But they applauded and I remember thinking this is definitely something I want to do one day."

'OTOLOSE AND SĀLONI MAEA

Two of the many heroes of the 2009 tsunami

Village: Falehau, Niuatoputapu

Niuatoputapu, Tafahi and Niuafo'ou are a group of islands known as the "Niuas", in the far north of the Tongan islands.

Before September 2009, about 950 people lived on Niuatoputapu in the three coastal villages of Hihifo, Falehau and Vaipoa; with another 70 in an elevated village on Tafahi Island. Their lifestyle depended on fishing, gardening and the weaving of pandanus to produce mats. The sea was an important part of their lives.

Niuatoputapu sits on the edge of the deep Tonga Trench, one of the most seismically active regions on earth. At 6:48am on 30 September, 2009, a powerful undersea earthquake caused a large tsunami that devastated the surrounding coastlines of American Samoa, Samoa and northern Tonga.

Three waves swept into Hihifo, Falehau and Vaipoa, with the third wave reportedly higher than the coconut trees on the beach. During the first and second smaller waves, many of the residents evacuated to higher places and were saved in spite of the devastation to their communities.

The tsunami killed 189 people; nine of them in Niuatoputapu. The people of the Niuas who witnessed the power of the tsunami will never forget that day.

'Otolose Maea (25) and her brother Sāloni (27), live with their grandparents on Niuatoputapu. Here's their account of what happened on that fateful day:

Sāloni was lying on his bed when the shaking started. 'Otolose felt the shaking too but didn't think it was anything to worry about. "I had just sat down to prepare tea when I heard a wave booming and then voices shouting," 'Otolose says.

"Run!" people were yelling. "There's a wave!"

Sāloni jumped from his bed and ran outside with his sister to see what was happening. To their horror, they saw a huge wave approaching.

"I'll get our bus," Sāloni said. "Get our grandparents ready by the door."

But that wouldn't be easy - their grandfather was in a wheelchair and it was usually a slow process to get him into the bus. 'Otolose feared the worst.

The bus was parked about 100 metres away. When Sāloni got to the bus, he was alarmed to find it packed with desperate women and children pleading with him to save them. Sāloni quickly started the bus and drove back to his grandparents' home.

The gigantic wave was rapidly approaching and the people in the bus yelled at 'Otolose to hurry and come. But 'Otolose knew there wouldn't be enough time to get her grandparents to the bus. She told them to go without her.

The people on the bus began screaming hysterically. The huge wave was nearly upon them. Sāloni was torn. What should he do – try to save his family, or drive the people in the bus to safety?

"Go!" 'Otolose yelled. "Get the people out of here!"

Leaving his family was the most heart wrenching thing Sāloni had ever done in his life.

'Otolose went back inside the house and helped her grandparents into the living room. "I had my grandfather seated in his wheelchair, and then my parents arrived," she says.

The family watched in terror as the oncoming wave swept up a house and a car and carried them straight toward their home. "I bowed with my eyes closed, knowing that we would not live," 'Otolose says. All they could do now was hold on to each other and wait for the worst to happen.

And then, a miracle …

Instead of crashing into the family's home, the tumbling house and car hit a *pua* tree and ricocheted off in another direction!

The relieved family managed to get out of the flooded house and joined the rest of the people of Niuatoputapu in the safety of higher ground. It was a tragedy that nine people lost their lives. But it could have been many more if not for the brave actions of 'Otolose and Sāloni.

NOTE

This account is based on interviews with survivors of the tsunami conducted by 'Anau Fonokalafi. The interviews were recorded in a book called *Niuatoputapu Tsunami: Tongan survivor accounts of the 2009 South Pacific earthquake and tsunami*. The book was co-published by the Tonga Broadcasting Commission and the International Tsunami Information Centre. Special thanks to Nanise Fifita for permission to use the material and Mary Lyn Fonua for the idea and images.

'Otolose's memory of the day the 2009 tsunami nearly destroyed his family.

LORD VE'EHALA

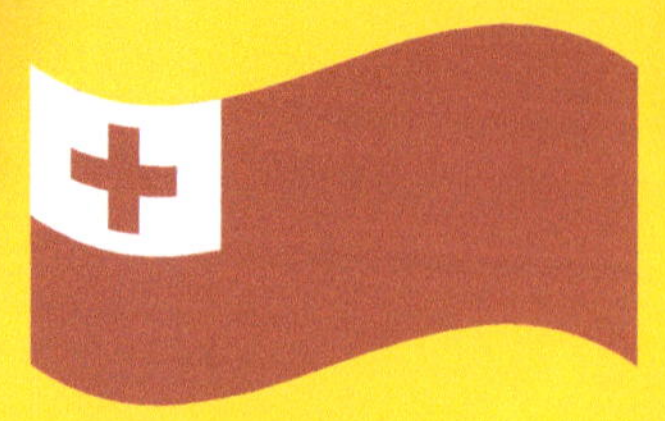

(1962-)
Brass band leader

Village: Fahefa

Ifi palasa (brass bands) are one of the most important musical forms in Tonga. Every high school has a brass band and more people play brass instruments than any other instrument in the kingdom.

The Royal Corps of Musicians for His Majesty's Armed Forces is the most prestigious brass band in Tonga. They are called upon to support the monarch during coronations, on the monarch's birthday, at independence celebrations and to welcome international delegates.

Lord Ve'ehala was the Director of Music of the Royal Corps of Musicians for almost twenty years.

Ve'ehala fell in love with brass bands the minute he first saw them as a child in the 1960s. He couldn't get enough of watching high school bands and the Tonga Police Band on parade.

He loved brass bands so much that his father bought him some audio cassettes of the Fiji Military Forces Band and the Queen's Regimental Bands to listen to.

In 1974, he joined the brass section in the 'Apifo'ou College band. He also learned how to read and write music.

Later, he went to St Patrick's College, Silverstream, in New Zealand to continue his education. He learned to play the trombone and joined the school orchestra. One of his favourite memories is the day his parents bought him a trombone so he could play at home.

In 1981, Ve'ehala joined the Tongan army because he wanted to serve his country. Crown Prince Tupouto'a (later King George Tupou V) was the Minister of Defence at the time and he established a brass band.

A member of The Royal Corps of Musicians for His Majesty's Armed Forces.

The purpose of the band was to provide musical support for the Royal Family, the government, the military and the community and to represent Tonga in overseas performances.

The Crown Prince saw potential in Ve'ehala to be a future leader of the band and sent him to Australia to study at the Defence Force School of Music.

Ve'ehala learned all the skills needed to lead a military brass band including administration and management.

He also developed his understanding of music theory and composition and learned to write music in styles as varied as anthems, big band, fanfare, hymns, marches, popular song and singing with accompaniment.

Ve'ehala graduated with a Bandmaster Certificate and with a Diploma of Applied Music and Music Management.

From 1987 to 2006, Ve'ehala led The Royal Corps of Musicians, a group of men who are soldiers and musicians. They represented Tonga throughout Australia, New Zealand and the Pacific.

They also performed in Germany, Switzerland and the USA and participated in the world famous Royal Edinburgh Military Tattoo multiple times.

"Every time we were asked to perform, whether locally or internationally, we brought our best performance," Ve'ehala says. "We wanted to show the people of Tonga and the rest of the world the great things we can do."

"When we travelled overseas we were ambassadors for our country. We did our best to represent Tonga and to represent Tongans living in the countries we visited. This is still the same with The Royal Corps of Musicians."

Lord Ve'ehala lived a dream he had his whole life and as an achiever he longs to see other people striving to be successful too.

His advice is simple: "Pursue the talent you were born to do," he says. "And when you've found it, stay focused on it."

IFI PALASA

Ifi palasa is the Tongan term for brass band, from the words *ifi* (to blow) and *palasa* (brass).

Brass instruments were first heard during Captain James Cook's voyages and are the oldest western form of music in Tonga.

In the mid nineteenth century, a German ship brought Tupou I's son home for burial. A German brass band played at the funeral and after this brass bands began to spread throughout the islands.

During World War Two, American soldiers used Tonga as a resting place. They introduced Tonga to instruments like saxophones and these have become part of modern *ifi palasa* as well.

The Royal Corps of Musicians play an important role during coronations.

THE SECRET CAVE

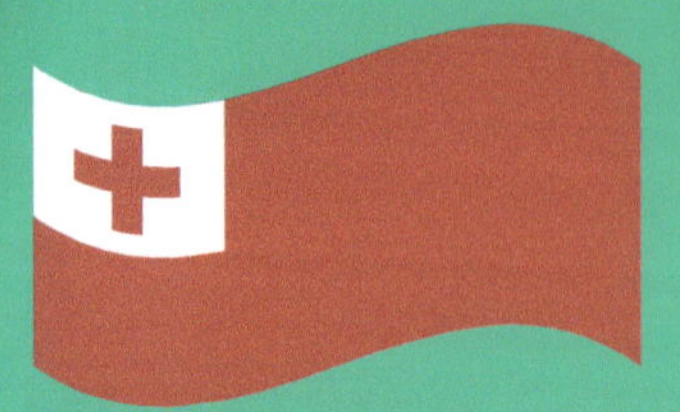

One Tu'i Vava'u was so mean to his people in ancient Tonga that a chief made a plan to kill him. When the Tu'i Vava'u discovered the plot, he vowed to drown the chief, his wife and daughter, 'Ofa, too.

A young man named Naua loved 'Ofa, but kept his love to himself because she was betrothed to another chief on the island. When he heard what the Tui Vava'u was going to do, he devised a plan to rescue her.

Naua had recently discovered a cave while he was hunting turtles. He didn't tell anyone about the cave because he had a feeling he might need a secret place of refuge one day.

He ran to 'Ofa's fale and finding her alone, asked her to come outside.

"Your life is in danger, but I've come to save you," he said.

'Ofa looked in Naua's eyes and saw genuine care. She held his hand as he led her through the forest behind the village. As they ran he told her what the Tu'i Vava'u was planning to do to her family.

Naua and 'Ofa emerged from the forest and on to a deserted beach where a canoe lay waiting. The canoe was filled with food and water supplies.

"Where are we going?" 'Ofa asked.

"I found a secret cave where you can hide until it's safe," Naua explained.

Naua paddled the canoe past some of the smaller islands near the reef. He stopped paddling when they arrived at a rock formation at the very edge of the islands.

"Follow me," he said and dived into the water.

'Ofa and Naua swam under a small ledge near the bottom of the rocks. The water here was cold and dark, but 'Ofa trusted Naua and held on to his feet as he swam.

They turned a corner, rose out of the water and into a cave.

Naua helped 'Ofa out of the water and on to a resting spot he had prepared in the cave. Then he showed her how to make fire for cooking food and staying warm.

The next morning he returned to Vava'u so that nobody would suspect anything.

During the day he sneaked away again and brought mats for 'Ofa to lie on, ngatu for clothing, and sandalwood oil for perfume. He wanted 'Ofa to be as comfortable as possible.

Later that day Naua made his confession.

"I have always loved you," he said. "But out of respect for your family I kept my love a secret."

"These circumstances mean I can be honest too," 'Ofa replied. "You who would risk his life for me, are the man who deserves my love and no other."

Once again, Naua had to leave his beloved and return to Vava'u in case someone wondered where he was. Naua promised this would be the last time he'd leave her.

"I'm going to Fiji," he told his friends later that day. "Come with me and bring your wives. Please don't say anything about this to anyone in case Tu'i Vava'u stops us."

They prepared a large canoe for the voyage and were just about to leave when one of Naua's friends challenged him.

"We're all taking our wives with us," he said. "Aren't you going to take a Tongan wife?"

"I'll find a wife on the way," he replied.

When the canoe was near the rock formation, Naua stood up. "Wait here," he told his friends as he dived into the water. "And I'll come back with a wife."

"What?" the others wondered. "Is he going crazy?"

Time passed and the friends began to worry about Naua. Had he been eaten by sharks? Was he playing some kind of trick on them? Just what was he up to?

Suddenly the water parted and Naua emerged ... with a young woman holding on to his back!

"Is she a goddess?" said one of the friends as he fell backwards in the canoe.

"No, that's the daughter of the chief's family that Tu'i Vava'u killed," said another. "That must be her ghost!"

Naua and 'Ofa climbed on board the canoe and Naua showed them that 'Ofa was neither a goddess nor a ghost.

He explained how he had saved her and hid her in the secret cave.

The group sailed on to Fiji and lived with a chief who looked after them.

At last, after two years, they received news that the Tu'i Vava'u had died and it was safe to return home, where they lived the rest of their lives in peace.

JONAH TALI LOMU

Village: Holopeka

He's had a photo shoot with Mariah Carey, judged a Miss World contest and had tea with the Queen of England ... but it's his deeds on the rugby field that Jonah Lomu is most known for. He's one of the most famous rugby players in history and while he lived, was beloved the world over.

Jonah was born in New Zealand but as a baby he was adopted by his aunty and uncle and taken to Holopeka, in the Ha'apai islands. Jonah loved his life in Tonga, surrounded by family, swimming every day and going to church.

When Jonah was six, his birth parents took him back to Mangere, South Auckland. Jonah struggled to adapt to life in New Zealand, especially at school. He couldn't speak English well and found it hard to make friends.

One thing Jonah enjoyed was sports. He played rugby league for the Manukau Magpies and was selected for representative teams. He loved athletics too and even won the Auckland Intermediate schools' high jump championship.

But life at home was tough. Jonah said his father was a hard worker and he admired that about him. But he also said his father drank a lot of alcohol and that he was violent.

As Jonah grew into a teenager, he spent more and more time away from home, often with friends and relatives who were in gangs. Sometimes they beat up other young people and took their clothes or their bikes. Occasionally, they stole cars.

Jonah was an angry person and got into lots of fights. "When I fought, I almost always thought of my father," he said. "I imagined that I was beating him up. Sometimes I would completely lose control – I didn't know when to stop."

One day, Jonah came home with bruises on his face and cuts on his arm from where he'd been stabbed with a broken beer bottle. His mother Hepi, knew she had to do something to save her son.

Jonah scored four tries to help the All Blacks
knock England out of the 1995 Rugby World Cup.

So she sent him to Wesley College, a boarding school in rural South Auckland.

Things didn't start well for Jonah at Wesley. He hit a student on his first day and had six detentions by the end of his second day. But teachers saw potential in Jonah and were patient with him, especially Deputy Principal, Chris Grinter.

Chris taught Jonah how to use his anger in positive ways. He bought a punching bag and set it up in a store room. "Whenever you feel like fighting someone, come and get this key off me," he said. "You can take your anger out on the bag!"

Chris was also the coach of the school rugby team and he selected Jonah for the First XV when Jonah was just fourteen years old! Did Jonah make a difference? Well, the team just happened to win the New Zealand schools championship that year!

Jonah made the New Zealand Secondary Schools team and some wealthy schools tried to entice him away from Wesley. But there was no way he was leaving – they may have had more resources, but they didn't have the care and support Jonah appreciated most of all.

In his last year of school, Jonah was named captain of the First XV and Head Boy of Wesley College. What an amazing turn around for a young man who just a few years earlier looked like he was heading for jail, and maybe an early death.

With Jonah as captain, Wesley won the national schools fifteens and sevens competitions. Once again he was picked in the New Zealand Secondary Schools team, playing alongside future All Blacks like Carlos Spencer and Christian Cullen.

At the end of the school year, Jonah played for Counties in the national sevens champs, the first time he had played against men in New Zealand. Counties won the competition and Jonah was named player of the tournament!

At just 18 years of age, Jonah was picked in the New Zealand sevens team and helped them win the famous Hong Kong sevens. Two months later he was an All Black! "When I heard my name read out I was ecstatic," Jonah

said. "I tried to look calm and composed but inwardly I wanted to jump up and scream and shout."

Jonah's first test match was against France on 26 June, 1994. He was only nineteen years old, the youngest test All Black in history. Jonah gave his first All Black jersey to his mother, Hepi.

Unfortunately, the test series didn't go well for Jonah or the All Blacks. Jonah had played loose forward all his life, but the All Blacks played him on the wing. The All Blacks lost both games and some commentators criticised the way Jonah played. He was sent back to Counties to learn more about playing winger.

"It was sad knowing I wasn't going to be part of the All Blacks," Jonah said. "I made a pledge to myself that next time I would be a more complete player."

Jonah's hard work paid off and in 1995 he made the All Blacks team to go to the Rugby World Cup in South Africa. He dominated the World Cup scoring tries no one had ever seen before, including length of the field, swerving, stepping tries scored with sheer speed; and bruising, bulldozing tries scored by sheer power!

He quickly became the most popular player at the World Cup. No longer could Jonah go into a shop to buy something like toothpaste. "The whole mall followed me!" he said. "Security had to escort me out back doors and down fire escapes."

Some people might think that kind of fame would be exciting, but Jonah didn't see it that way. "It was scary, especially being so young," he said. "The hardest part was that I didn't have anyone to talk to about it because no one had gone through that."

For the next seven years, Jonah dominated international rugby and became a global superstar. Many people believe he changed rugby by bringing commercial attention to the game in ways it had never experienced before.

Behind the scenes however, Jonah was fighting an opponent stronger than any player he had faced.

In 1996, Jonah was diagnosed with nephrotic syndrome, a rare form of kidney disease. Some doctors said he might have to retire from rugby. Jonah was a very humble person and decided not to tell people about his illness. "He looks

tired out there," critics said. "And why has he put on so much weight?" They didn't know it was caused by the medication he was taking.

Jonah tried to stay positive. "I never got to the stage of feeling sorry for myself," he said. "The tougher things got the more I thought about those people less fortunate than me."

Jonah's kidney illness eventually forced him to retire early from rugby. He played sixty three tests, and scored thirty seven tries for the All Blacks in his career.

Things may not have ended well in rugby but they did in Jonah's family life. One day he visited his parents' home and saw his father gardening. "When he saw me he began crying," Jonah said. "He said, 'I thought I would die without ever seeing you again.' We hugged and we both cried."

Though he's known mostly for what he did in the black jersey, Jonah never forgot his roots. "I'm proud to say I'm a New Zealand-born Tongan," he said. "I represent two countries."

Jonah passed away suddenly in November 2015. He was only 40 years old. Jonah is survived by his wife Nadene, and sons Brayley and Dhyreille.

TONGAN ALL BLACKS

The first All Black of Tongan descent was Walter Batty, who was born in Tonga in 1905. Walter played six matches (four tests) for New Zealand between 1928 and 1931. Malakai Fekitoa is a recent All Black who hails from Tonga. Malakai was born in Ha'apai but first started playing rugby at Liahona High School on Tongatapu. He played sevens for Tonga as a teenager and came to New Zealand after he won a scholarship to attend the same school Jonah went to – Wesley College.

DR KONAI HELU THAMAN

(1946-)
Poet

Village: Kolomotu'a

Dr Konai Helu Thaman is an academic, an educator and a poet. She's one of the most influential Pacific writers and has five collections of poetry to her name.

Konai was born in Nuku'alofa, the eldest of four children. She attended Free Wesleyan Primary and later, Tonga High School. Konai worked hard at school and was rewarded with a scholarship to study at Epsom Girls' Grammar School in Auckland.

It wasn't easy for a young person to leave Tonga and go to a foreign place in those days. Konai had to learn a new language, learn how to cope in a western education system and learn how to deal with people who didn't see the world like she did. Sometimes she felt lonely and missed the familiar lifestyle she knew in Tonga.

But Konai's hard work paid off and she eventually earned three university degrees, became Professor of Pacific Education and Culture at USP (Fiji) and the UNESCO Chairperson in Teacher Education and Culture. Talk about a scholar!

As well as being an academic, Konai is an accomplished writer and poet. She's written numerous scholarly articles and published five collections of poetry: You the Choice of My Parents (1974), Langakali (1981), Hingano (1987), Kakala (1993) and Songs of Love (1999).

One of Konai's favourite subjects is the beauty of Tongan culture and traditions. Sometimes people think these have no value in modern life. Konai doesn't think that way.

Must you throw this medicinal branch
Out the door?
It will put out roots
And one day the tree will destroy
Your brick house
You, and your sick son.
(Langakali)

Teaching a group of educators at Tonga Teachers' College.

As Tonga came into contact with the western world in the twentieth century, it went through dramatic changes. Some of Konai's poems look at what has been "lost" during this time.

The embers wait
Perhaps never to be
Rekindled by
Dry coconut leaves
… kerosene is easier!

(Island Fire)

As well as lamenting the loss of some aspects of Tongan traditions, Konai also writes poems that challenge her culture. One of her most famous poems tells the thoughts of a woman forced into an arranged marriage.

I see myself dying slowly
To family and traditions;
Stripped of its will and carefree spirit,
Naked on the cold and lonely waters
Of a strange family shoreline
Alienated from belonging truly.

(You the Choice of My Parents)

A feature of Konai's style is the use of Pacific imagery, especially Tongan trees, plants and flowers. She uses these to symbolise the beauty of Tongan customs.

Many of the poems in Kakala reflect this idea. A kakala is a necklace of perfumed flowers and leaves given to visitors. Songs and poems are often described as hiva kakala – love songs to be given away.

come
take this kakala
sacred symbol of our oneness
tie it tightly around you
where it will remain fresh
in the nourishing flow
only the sky knows

(Kakala Folau)

Konai uses poetry to share the beauty and challenges of being Tongan with the world. It's one of the ways she honours her culture. "We should always value and respect our traditions and treat them as privileges," she says.

"Being Tongan gives me a foundation. It provides me with traditional knowledge and values which I use in my personal and professional life. And it gives me the opportunity to identify and share with other Pacific Island people."

Konai knows what it takes to be successful and she has simple advice for young people who want to follow in her footsteps. "Work hard and don't give up easily," she says. "Be humble and have *'ofa*, (compassion and kindness)."

POETRY IN ANCIENT TONGA

Poets were highly regarded in ancient Tonga and poems were often given as precious gifts. Most poetry was either sung or chanted and many had dance movements accompanying them.

The most talented composers are punake – composers of dance, music and poetry. High ranking chiefs often had their own punake, dancers and musicians.

If a man wanted to court a woman, he would find a composer to write a song for her. If she accepted the song, she would reply with one of her own. Loka Siliva, the song Queen Salote wrote for Viliami Tungī Mailefihi, is one of the most famous examples of this tradition.

SOPOLEMALAMA FILIPE TOHI

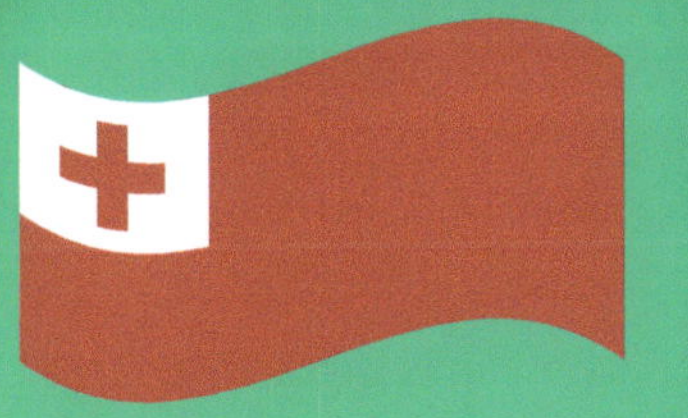

(1959-)
Artist

Villages: Fasi, Ngele'ia, Kolofo'ou

Filipe Tohi is a world famous, award winning artist whose work is found in places as diverse as China, England, France, Japan and even Saudi Arabia! He's a drawer, sculptor, painter, carver, photographer, and videographer … when it comes to visual arts, there's nothing this talented son of Tonga can't do!

Filipe's grandmother Louveve, was a weaver and tapa maker and Filipe loved to help her cut and prepare *loa kau* (flax) that she would weave into mats and other items. Filipe remembers warm Pacific nights, drifting in and out of sleep while his grandmother wove her magic next to him.

Something of Louveve's creativity flowed into her grandson. Filipe loved to draw and sometimes that love took over everything else in his life. "I used to run away from school to draw in the bush," he says.

One time a teacher checked his book for homework but instead of spelling and punctuation exercises, she found pages filled with sketches of birds, plants and people. She marched him straight to the Headmaster.

"This boy is wasting time with all this drawing and needs to be punished," she said.

The Headmaster flicked through Filipe's books, nodding seriously. Filipe waited to be told he was being sent home and thought about what he was going to say to his family. They'd be disappointed. "Your education is very important," they always said. "Treat these books and materials we give you with respect because they cost money and they will help you have a good future."

The Headmaster lay Filipe's books on the table, then pointed to a framed photo on his desk. It was a picture of the Headmaster holding his cat. "Would you draw this for me?" he asked. When Filipe finished the drawing he was sent back to class.

Later that day Filipe was called to the front of the school assembly. "Oh no, this must be the time I'm going to be punished," he thought.

"This boy wins the award for *Most Talented Student*," the Headmaster declared, handing Filipe a certificate as the whole school clapped. "He's an artist!"

Filipe says he didn't really understand what, "He's an artist" meant. He only knew that it felt good to be recognised and rewarded for things he loved to do.

Filipe even found ways to get paid for his talents. He made stencils from the covers of exercise books and used them to print designs on his friends' tee shirts. His most popular prints were of ABBA, Bruce Lee, hibiscus flowers and other Tongan images and patterns. In return, his "customers" bought him movie tickets and ice creams.

Filipe's family moved to New Zealand when he was eighteen and he found work as a labourer. His workmates wore plain tee shirts to work, but that was impossible for Filipe. He couldn't look at a shirt without wanting to put a design on it, even if all he had to use were felt tip marker pens.

"You're an artist, bro," his workmates would say, admiring his latest designs.

"There's that word 'artist' again," Filipe thought to himself. "I still don't know what it means, but people seem to like what I do."

Not long after this, the family moved to New Plymouth and Filipe found a way to grow his passion. He began studying at the Rangimarie Arts and Crafts Institute, a school that taught Maori carving.

"Spending so much time with Maori people was so good for me," Filipe says. "The way they spoke and chanted reminded me of my grandmother."

As well as carving, Filipe painted and drew pictures of wildlife, the landscape and important people in his life, just as he'd done in Tonga.

Teachers at the school praised Filipe's work and he was even hired as a tutor. But one day an older Tongan artist said something that challenged him. "There's more to art than this you know," he said while examining one of Filipe's favourite pieces.

"I make lashing designs in patterns that people are familiar with. But I might use aluminium or iron or cut them into stone."

It was the first time anyone had said anything critical about his work. "It made me angry at first," he admits. "But it was good that he said that. Sometimes you think you know everything, but you don't, and it's good to learn that so you can be more open."

Filipe says an important moment in his life was when he learned about "lashing". Some people asked him to lash a special canoe for a museum and gave him some books containing drawings of traditional lashing techniques.

He experimented with different kinds of lashing styles of his own, mixing them with tapa patterns and other Tongan designs.

"I like the patterns the lashings make because they remind me of how Pacific people are connected," he says. "The rope is like an umbilical cord that binds canoes and houses and people together."

By combining ancient Tongan designs with modern carving, pottery and sculpture and non-traditional materials, Filipe helps to keep these connections alive.

"I make lashing designs in patterns that people are familiar with," he says. "But I might use aluminium or iron or cut them into stone. That leads people to ask questions, so the pieces are like a bridge for them to learn more about their identity, especially for those born outside of the islands."

Filipe used to wonder what it meant when people called him an "artist". Maybe it's someone who uses creative ways to connect people to each other and to their true selves.

And maybe that's why people love Filipe's work so much … and not just Pacific people. His art has been exhibited all around the world and he's been commissioned to make pieces in New Zealand, Fiji, Tonga, Japan, and China.

If this story inspires you to find your passion, Filipe has a simple word of advice: "The more you do something, the better you'll become and doors will open," he says.

"I loved art from when I was a child and I stuck with it. It's like learning to ride a bike. You fall down many times, but if you keep getting up and trying again you learn how to ride and then you can go anywhere. Good things take time."

Did you know?

- Filipe received his Samoan title, Sopolemalama, from Tui Atua Tupua Tamasese Tā'isi Efi, the Head of State of Samoa.

- Filipe's son, Solo, is a member of the Australian boy band, Justice Crew. They've won awards for their work with Justin Bieber and Chris Brown.

- You can see more of Filipe's work at his website http://www.lalava.net/

THE UNIQUENESS OF TONGAN ART

Dagmar Dyck and Ruha Fifita are Tongan artists who enjoy mixing traditional Tongan design with modern materials and images.

Dagmar was the first Tongan female to graduate from the respected Elam School of Fine Arts. "A lot of my work is based on *koloa*," Dagmar says. "I really like the patterns they make. Tongan art is very stylistic."

Ruha Fifita was born in Neiafu, Vava'u. Ruha is most known for the unique *ngatu* she creates with New Zealand artist Dame Robin White and women in Tonga. "Making ngatu is a deeply rooted cultural practise," Ruha says. "Our Tongan-ness is honoured in creating these large scale ngatu works."

An installation by Filipe combining lalava (lashing) patterns
and techniques with non-traditional materials.

EPELI HAU'OFA

Epeli Hau'ofa was a scholar, writer and one of the greatest thinkers in Pacific history.

Epeli's parents were missionaries and he was born on a mission station in Papua New Guinea. He was fascinated by the cultures of the different Papua New Guinean tribes he came into contact with. He enjoyed learning the languages and customs of other ethnic groups.

This continued as Epeli went through his childhood education. He was comfortable with people from different cultures and enjoyed finding things in common between Tongan culture and the people he met as his family travelled around the Pacific.

When he finished high school, Epeli went to Australia to study and met his wife Barbara.

Next, Epeli's journeys took him to McGill University in Montreal, Canada to do his Masters degree. He did the fieldwork for his degree on the islands of Trinidad and Tobago in the Caribbean Sea.

From 1978 to 1981, he served as the Deputy Private Secretary to the late King of Tonga, Keeper of the Palace Records and Secretary of the Tongan Traditions Committee. If anyone knew about Tongan culture and history, it was Epeli!

In 1983, Epeli joined the USP campus in Fiji and became the head of various departments. In 1997, he achieved one of his greatest life goals when he became the first Director of the Oceania Centre for Arts and Culture.

The Oceania Centre was created to help look after and develop Pacific cultural knowledge in the university. The centre is world famous for its art, dance and music programs.

Epeli believed that the common heritage of Pacific people was special and he was sad that people sometimes focussed more on differences between Pacific peoples than the things they share in common.

"Nineteenth century imperialism erected boundaries that led to the contraction of Oceania," he wrote, "transforming a once boundless world into the Pacific states and territories we know today."

"Fiji, Samoa, Tonga, Niue, Rotuma, Tokelau, Tuvalu, Futuna and Uvea formed a large exchange community in which wealth and people with their skills and arts, circulated endlessly."

One writer described Epeli as "a true Pacific man". Maybe that's because he travelled through the Pacific so much as he was growing up and had a bigger view of want it means to be a Pacific Islander than someone who grows up in one place.

He hoped that Pacific people would maintain the relationships they had known with each other for centuries. He felt that not only would that enrich the Pacific world but would help protect it from outside forces.

"Acting together as a region, for the interests of the region as a whole, and above those of our individual countries, would enhance our chances for survival," he wrote.

Epeli refused to describe Pacific Islands as "small" because he felt that led to negative thinking. He argued the Pacific is the home of people who think and dream big.

"When those who hail from continents see a Polynesian or Micronesian island they naturally pronounce it small or tiny," he said. "Their calculation is based entirely on the extent of the land surfaces that they see."

"But if we look at the myths, legends and oral traditions of the peoples of Oceania, they did not conceive of their world in such microscopic proportions."

"Their universe comprised the surrounding ocean, the underworld with its fire-controlling and earth-shaking denizens, and the heavens above with their hierarchies of powerful gods and named stars and constellations that people could count on to guide their ways across the seas. Their world was anything but tiny."

He referred to characters from Pacific legends who performed amazing feats, like Muni Matamahae of Tonga, Laufoli of Niue and Sinilau of Samoa.

"One legendary Oceanic athlete was so powerful that during a competition he threw his javelin with such force that it pierced the horizon and disappeared until that night, when it was seen streaking across the skyline like a meteor," Epeli wrote.

"Every now and then it reappears to remind people of the mighty deed. And as far as I'm concerned it is still out there, near Jupiter or somewhere. That was the first ever rocket sent into space."

Professor Epeli Hau'ofa passed away in 2009 but his ideas about life in the Pacific inspire many to this day.

NGAOHI FANGUFANGU

Dr 'Okusitino Māhina is a Tongan social anthropologist who is helping to revive traditional fangufangu (Tongan nose flutes). "These art forms are slowly disappearing," says Dr. Māhina. Scan the QR code below to watch *Tufunga Ngaohifungafunga* - a film about the nose flute revival by New Zealand film maker, Paul Janman.

KAMELIA LINO ZARKA

(1961-)
Pilot

Villages: Kolofo'ou, Fasi, Houmakelikao.

Kamelia Zarka was the first Tongan woman to reach the rank of Captain on a commercial airline.

Kamelia was born in Kolofo'ou, Tongatapu. She went to the Government Primary School in Fasi and later attended St. Andrew's High School and Tonga High School in Nuku'alofa.

In her last year of school, Kamelia travelled to Norway as an exchange student. "What an exciting experience that was," she says. "Everything was so different to what I was used to - the culture, weather, people, language, food ...There were seven Tongan students which turned out to be a great support system for all of us. I learned how to ski in Norway!"

She also spent time working for the Red Cross organisation in Spain and Switzerland.

Travelling through Europe opened Kamelia's eyes to the world of flying and the exciting possibilities there were to see the world.

When she returned to Tonga, Kamelia worked as the Youth Coordinator for the Tongan Red Cross for seven years before meeting her future husband, Christopher Zarkas, who was a Peace Corps Volunteer.

In 1992, Kamelia and her family moved to Hawaii and Kamelia began work as a flight attendant on Hawaiian Airlines. Lots of Polynesian women choose that occupation – it's glamourous and interesting work. But Kamelia wanted more.

One day on a flight to American Samoa, Kamelia had the opportunity to sit at the front of the plane in the cockpit. She watched the pilots as they worked on the flight instruments, spoke to air control and negotiated the plane through turbulence. "I could do that," she thought to herself.

No obstacle was going to stop Kamelia from achieving her dream
of being the first Tongan woman to Captain a commercial airline.

She went home that day and told her husband that she no longer wanted to serve people in planes. She wanted to fly the planes!

So what did this high achieving Tongan do next? She enrolled in flight schools in Hawaii and Oklahoma, USA, that's what!

There were a lot of challenges that Kamelia had to overcome on her journey to becoming a pilot. The fees were expensive and studying took a lot of her family time. One of the biggest obstacles was a lack of female support and role models.

"Sometimes people around me were negative," Kamelia says. "They'd tell me it was a waste of time and that no one would hire me. But I didn't pay attention to them because I knew in my heart that I would achieve my goal. I talked back with my actions by proving them all wrong."

Kamelia also relied on her faith in God and her family's encouragement to help her get through these times. "Of course, no journey is easy," she says. "There were times when only this support and the belief in myself and my skills allowed me to continue on this journey."

Kamelia worked slowly toward her goal. She began as a flight instructor, teaching students how to fly in Michigan, USA. Next she became a Flight Engineer, then a Second Officer on a DC10 and then a First Officer on a Boeing 767.

Finally, in 2009, she reached her goal - Captain on a Boeing 717!

"Every airline pilot aims to be a Captain and I was so excited to reach that rank," Kamelia says. "It's challenging though, because it comes with a lot of responsibility. It's my name on all the paperwork and if something goes wrong, I take the blame."

"But it's good that the Captain is not alone," Kamelia continues. "I have the First Officer and the Flight Attendants and we all work together toward a common goal: to get everyone safely to their destinations."

Kamelia flies the inter-island routes, taking up to a thousand passengers a day. What does she love about her job? "Being able to watch the sunrise every morning from the best seat in the plane," she says, "And then following that by greasing a landing."

One of the great things about Kamelia's achievements is they give her the opportunity to represent Tonga. "The Tongan culture is like music to my soul," she says. "I speak, read and write in Tongan. I enjoy our ceremonial events and I proudly talk about Tonga to anyone who wants to know about my culture and people."

"To me being Tongan means being an ambassador for my God, my King and my country."

Kamelia's achievements are evidence that Tongan young people can achieve any goal they dream of … even if no one else has done it before.

"Dreams become reality when you start working towards them," she says. "Don't sit and talk about them. Nike says it best: 'JUST DO IT!' Don't listen to the negatives. The negative things that people said to me were my fuel. Negativity made me stronger because in my heart I knew I would prove them wrong."

Whatever your dreams are in life, Kamelia encourages you to do all you can to fulfil them. "Come join me," she says, "the view is incredible."

SHE GOES UP, THEY GO DOWN

Kamelia's eldest daughter Maria Zarka, is a Tongan achiever herself. Maria is a four time NCAA Division III diving champion and represented Tonga in diving at the 2014 Commonwealth Games in Glasgow. Her sister Kaimana Zarka is a promising diver as well.

'Come join me, the view is incredible!"

YOUR TURN

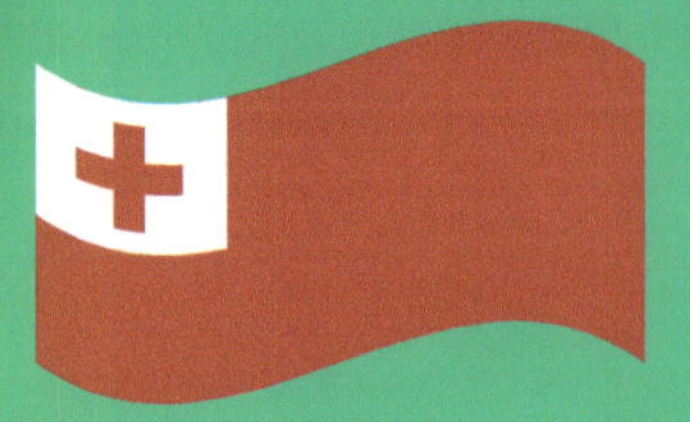

Use this book as a starting point to do your own research on Tongan achievers.

You could find out about:

- Basketballer Jabari Parker who was the second player picked in the 2014 NBA draft.
- Dr 'Ana Taufe'ulungaki, the first woman Minister of Education in Tonga.
- Pioneering health professional Dr. Leopino Foliaki.
- Award-winning playwright, Suli Moa.
- Mina Wharepouri, the first Tongan born judge in New Zealand.
- Architect and architectural researcher, Charmaine 'Ilaiu Talei.
- Dr. Tu'uhevaha Kaitu'u Lino, an inspirational award-winning scientist.

You could ask family members to tell you stories about their achievements.

You're an achiever too.

In your life you have already accomplished many of the goals you set for yourself.

Let the stories in this book inspire you to achieve even more!

"Tō ē to'a kae tu'u ē to'a."

"Lusia ki taulanga."

SOURCES AND NOTES

See also the Bibliography on page 129. It contains full details of the publications recorded below.

The First Tongans
This is an adaptation of creation stories recorded in Rutherford, Friendly Islands.

King George Tupou I
Information in this chapter comes from articles by Adrienne L. Kaeppler and Sione Latukefu in Wood-Ellem, Tonga and the Tongans.

Polynesian Cultural Centre, "The King of Tonga George Tupou I", Polynesian Cultural Centre, Retrieved from https://www.youtube.com/watch?v=vZU_PlzKbV0.

"The socio-economic …" Latukefu p4.

Valerie Adams
NZOC staff, "Emotional gold medal ceremony," September 21, 2012, http://www.olympic.org.nz/news/emotional-gold-medal-ceremony.

Ben Stanley, "Wake up call golden for Adams' family," Fairfax Media, August 15, 2012,

http://www.stuff.co.nz/sport/olympics/track-field/7478628/Wake-up-call-golden-for-Adams-family

Eugene Bingham, "A throwback to the past," NZ Herald, August 18, 2004.

Eugene Bingham, "Valerie Vili - two shots, one aim," NZ Herald July15, 2006.

Olympic.org staff, "Valerie Adams," http://www.london2012.com/athlete/adams-valerie-1125260/.

"It's unusual …" Andrew Alderson, "Chief Valerie," Herald on Sunday, January 11, 2015.

"Looking up …" Paea Wolfgram, "Salvation in Sevens?" Spasifik, September/October 2012.

His Brother's Keeper
This is an adaptation of a story recorded in Craig, Handbook of Polynesian Mythology and Gifford, Tongan Myths and Tales. There are other versions of this story.

Queen Salote Tupou III
Most of the information in this chapter comes from Hixon, Salote, Queen of Paradise. Other information comes from Wood-Ellem, Tonga and the Tongans; and Helu, On Tongan Poetry.

"Everyone and no one …" Hixon p77.

"I am deeply sensible …" Hixon p78.

"I'm the only one …" Hixon p119.

"You lay down …" Hixon p140.

"The real essence …" Hixon p186.

"is one of the greatest …" Helu p39.

Loka Siliva .Hixon p68.

Dr Viliami Tangi
Most of the information in this chapter comes from Beckford and Fitzsimons, Navigators.

"It seemed impossible …" Beckford and Fitzsimons p10

Government of Tonga staff, "Lord Tangi of Vaonukonuka," December 30, 2010, http://www.mic.gov.to/government/nobles-of-the-realm/1969-lord-tangi-of-vaonukonuka.

Dr. Viliami Tangi, "Viliami Tangi," https://www.linkedin.com/in/viliami-tangi-1b69842a

Info about Dr Karlo Mila comes from Facebook correspondence with the author, April, 2016.

"Having Tongan ancestry …" Le Va staff, "Dr Karlo Mila," http://www.leva.co.nz/about/our-people/dr-karlo-mila

The First Tu'i Tonga
This is an adaptation of a story recorded In Rutherford, Friendly Islands. There are other versions of this story.

Information on ancient Tongan games comes from William Mariner's descriptions in An Account of the Natives of the Tonga Islands. In December 1806, an English ship visited Haapai. Most of the crew were killed by locals. William Mariner was a teenage boy on the ship. He was adopted by Finau, the high chief of Haapai. William lived in Tonga for four years before returning home to England. The story of his time in Tonga was recorded by John Martin a few years later.

Pita Vi
Information in this chapter comes from Statham, A History of Tonga; and Wood-Ellem, Tonga and the Tongans.

Haloti Ngata
"the size/speed ratio …" Bitonti, "Who is Haloti Ngata?" Draft Daddy, October 1, 2006, http://web.archive.org/web/20060618021500/http://www.draftdaddy.com:80/prospects/halotiNgata.cfm

"This is my uncle …" Kevin Van Valkenburg, "Sense of loss drives Ravens' Haloti Ngata," The Baltimore Sun, September 10, 2006,

http://www.baltimoresun.com/sports/ravens/bal-kvv-haloti-ngata-020512-story.html.

"I started thanking God…" Ibid.

"He was my best friend…" Ibid.

The Legend of the Scar Faced Orphan Hero
This is an adaptation of a story recorded in Craig, Handbook of Polynesian Mythology and Gifford, Tongan Myths and Tales. There are other versions of this story.

Professor 'Ilaisa Futa 'I Ha'angana Helu
Much of the information in this chapter comes from the film Tongan Ark directed by Paul Janman.

Emeline Afeaki-Mafileo
Much of the information in this chapter comes from an interview by the author, February 2016.

"My grandma …" Virginia Winder, "Mentor draws on Tongan roots," Taranaki Daily News, September 11, 2012,http://www.stuff.co.nz/taranaki-daily-news/features/7650326/Mentor-draws-on-Tongan-roots.

Inspiring Stories, "Emeline Afeaki Mafile'o – Speaking at FFTF14," Retrieved from https://vimeo.com/106121816.

Annah Stretton, "Emeline Afeaki-Mafile'o: I Am An Entrepreneur," Annah Stretton Unlimited, November 9, 2012, http://annahstrettonunlimited.com/2012/11/09/i-am-an-entrepreneur/.

A Polynesian Love Story
This is an adaptation of a story recorded in Luomala, Vices on the Wind and Gifford, Tongan Myths and Tales. There are other versions of this story. Katherine Luomala's book has an interesting comparison of Hina and Sinilau stories across Polynesia.

"It is quite likely …" Helu p55.

Tonga "Haku" Fifita
WWE staff, "Haku," WWE, http://www.wwe.com/superstars/haku.

Dwayne Johnson, "Uncle Tonga," 18 December, 2015, Retrieved from https://twitter.com/TheRock.

Information on ancient Tongan martial arts can be found in An Account of the Natives of the Tonga Islands by William Mariner.

The story of the Moa Uli was told by Reverend Tevita Finau in the following You Tube file:

Museum of New Zealand Te Papa Tongarewa, "Kava Clubs and Black Fowls - Tales from Te Papa episode 120," October 24, 2011, Retrieved from https://www.youtube.com/watch?v=gi2nAUURHjI.

"One could not wish …" Rutherford p89.

Hon. 'Akilisi Pohiva
Information from Island Kingdom by Ian Campbell.

Tagata Pasifika, "Tongan Prime Minister 'Akilisi Pohiva," Tagata Pasifika, February 6, 2015, Retrieved from https://www.youtube.com/watch?v=14wS-ArVUC0.

Tonga Prime Minister's Office staff, "Meet the Prime Minister of Tonga," February 2015, http://www.pmo.gov.to/.

Kalafi Moala, "'Akilisi Pohiva's long, hazardous road from chief critic to Tonga's new PM," Pacific Media Centre, January 7, 2015,http://www.pmc.aut.ac.nz/articles/akilisi-pohiva-long-hazardous-road-chief-critic-tongas-new-pm.

Kalino Latu, "New MP Jenny Salesa honours Tongan heritage," NZ Kaniva Pacific, October 23, 2014,   http://nzkanivapacific.co.nz/2014/10/new-mp-jenny-salesa-honours-tongan-heritage/.

The First Kava Circle

The legend is an adaptation of a story recorded in Gifford, Tongan Myths and Tales. There are other versions of this story. Information about the practise of giving kava to visiting ships comes from Rutherford, Friendly Islands.

Vili Nosa and Malakai Ofanoa, "The social, cultural and medicinal use of Kava for

twelve Tongan born men living in Auckland,NZ," Pacific Health Dialog Vol.15 No. 1, 2009, http://www.tepou.co.nz/uploads/files/resource-assets/the-social-cultural-and-medicinal-use-of-kava-for-twelve-tongan-born-men-living-in-new-zealand.pdf.

Sister Malia Tuifu'a

Information in this chapter comes from Adrienne Kaeppler's 2014 article in the Journal of the Polynesian Society volume 123, number 2. That issue of the JPS features articles on the lives of six extraordinary Polynesian women.

"I wanted to do something…" Beckford and Fitzsimons p83.

John Tui

Information comes from an interview by the author, February 2016, and the following articles:

New Idea staff, "John Tui," New Idea, May 1, 2012, https://nz.lifestyle.yahoo.com/new-idea/star-watch/article/-/13564688/john-tui/.

"It was a dream …" Lydia Jenkin, "Going great guns," Time Out. April 5-11, 2012.

"Once you get down …" Mema Maeli, "The Battle To Live The Dream," Spasifik May/June 2012

"To be the first Tongan …" Ibid.

"I just want to show …" Ibid.

"I've always been …" Tom Cardy, "Battleship Kiwi in Hollywood haka," The Dominion Post, April 5, 2012, http://www.stuff.co.nz/entertainment/film/6694790/Battleship-Kiwi-in-Hollywood-haka

Info about the Naufahu brothers comes from Facebook correspondence with the author, April 2016.

Marvel Universe of Tonga

The legend is an adaptation of a story recorded in Reed, Myths and Legends of Polynesia.

Hon. Baron Vaea

The Telegraph staff, "Baron Vaea of Houma," The Telegraph, September 11, 2009, http://www.telegraph.co.uk/news/obituaries/politics-obituaries/6175398/Baron-Vaea-of-Houma.html.

Matangi Tonga staff, "Baron Vaea passes away after a long life of service," Matangi Tonga, June 8, 2009, http://matangitonga.to/2009/06/08/baron-vaea-passes-away-after-long-life-service.

Sarah Chandler, "The two Vaeas: Tongan Prime Minister and RNZAF pilot," Royal New Zealand Air Force, http://www.airforce.mil.nz/about-us/news/feature-stories/feature-story-readonly.htm@guid=%7B66df0b7b-9d39-404b-b306-184f611cdb07%7D.htm.

Manu Vatuvei

Much of the information in this chapter comes from an interview by the author, April 2016.

No Mean Feet

The legend is an adaptation of a story recorded in Collacott, Tales and Poems of Tonga.

The Jets

Much of the information in this chapter comes from an interview by the author, January 2016.

Other information is from The Jets' official website http://www.thejetsband.com.

Information on Dinah Jane Hansen comes from Fifth Harmony's official website http://fifthharmonyofficial.com/.

Information about Lord Ve'ehala comes from e mail correspondence with the author, January 2016.

'Otolose and Sāloni Maea

This account is based on interviews by 'Anau Fonokalafi recorded in a book called Niuatoputapu Tsunami: Tongan survivor accounts of the 2009 South Pacific earthquake and tsunami.

Lord Ve'ehala

Information in this chapter comes from e mail correspondence with the author, April 2016.

Additional information comes from an interview by the author with Dr. Adrienne Kaeppler, March 2016.

The Secret Cave

The story is an adaptation of a version recorded by William Mariner.

Jonah Lomu

Most of the information in this chapter comes from Jonah's autobiography Jonah My Story.

"When I fought ..." Ibid p32.

"When I heard ..." Ibid p61.

"It was sad ..." Ibid p67.

"I never ..." Ibid p322.

"He gave ..." New Zealand Herald staff, "All Blacks legend Jonah Lomu dies aged 40," New Zealand Herald, November 18, 2015.

Lindsay Knight, "Jonah Lomu #941," New Zealand Rugby Museum, http://stats.allblacks.com/asp/profile.asp?ABID=506

"Pacific Warmth Captures Jonah," by Innes Logan in Spasifik, September/October 2011

Dr Konai Helu Thaman

Much of the information comes from e mail correspondence with the author, January 2016.

Other information comes from an article by Briar Wood, "Heka He Va'a Mei Popo," http://www.wsanz.org.nz/journal/docs/WSJNZ222Wood1998.pdf.

Sopolemalama Filipe Tohi

Information comes from an interview with the author, April 2016.

Information about Dagmar Dyck comes from Dagmar's official website http://dagmardyck.com.

Information about Ruha Fifita comes from e mail correspondence with the author, January 2016.

Epeli Hau'ofa

"We have to ..." Hau'ofa p23.

"When those who ..." Hau'ofa p31.

Kamelia Lino Zarka

Information comes from e mail correspondence with the author, April 2016.

PICTURE CREDITS

Alexander Turnbull Library 25, 27

International Olympic Committee 18, 19, 20

Methodist Collection, Drew University Library, USA ... 24

World Health Organisation 28,31

Matangi Tonga 29, 80, 95, 97, 98

David Hobby 40

Kevin Moore 41

Bill Hunter 42

Paul Janman 48, 49, 51

Emeline Afeaki-Mafile'o 52, 53, 55

United Nations Photos 63, 64

Parliamentarians for Global Action 65

Polynesian Society 70, 71, 72

Karen Kay Management 73

Eva Rinaldi 75

Air Force Museum of New Zealand 81, 82

Gettys 83, 84, 107

Rugby League Week 87

The Jets 92, 93, 94

US Marine Corps, Pacific 99, 101

Thibaut Plaire 106

Global Sports Forum 109

Dr. Konai Helu Thaman 110, 111, 112

Filipe Tohi 114, 115

Shannon McGee 117

Oceania Centre for Arts, Culture and Pacific Studies . 118

University of Hawaii Press 119

Kamelia Lino Zarka 120, 123

BIBLIOGRAPHY

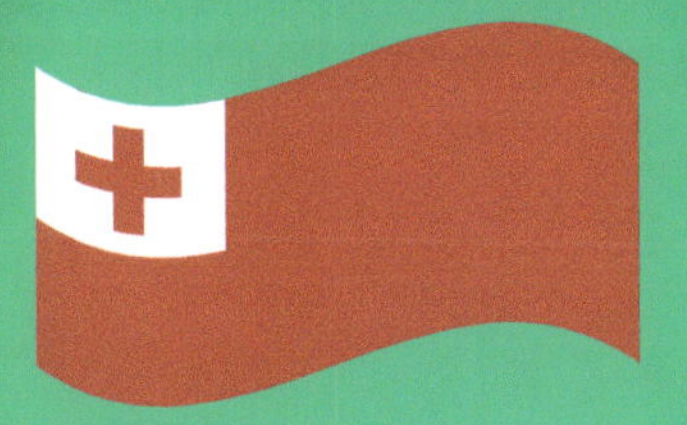

Beckford, Nigel and Fitzsimons, Mike. (2010). *Navigators*. Pasifika Medical Association in association with Fitzbeck Publishing: Auckland.

Benson, Eugene and Conolly, L.W. eds. (2005). *Encyclopedia of Post-Colonial Literatures in English*. Routledge: New York

Campbell, Ian C. (2015). *Island Kingdom*. Canterbury University Press: Christchurch

Collocott, E. E. V. (1928). *Tales and Poems of Tonga*. Bernice P. Bishop Museum: Honolulu, Hawaii

Craig, Robert D. (2004). *Handbook of Polynesian Mythology*. ABC-CLIO: Santa Barbara

Gifford, E.W. (1924). *Tongan Myths and Tales*. Bernice P. Bishop Museum: Honolulu, Hawaii

Helu, I. Futa. (2012). *On Tongan Poetry*. Atuanui Press: Auckland

Hau'ofa, Epeli. (2008). *We Are the Ocean*. University of Hawaii Press: Honolulu

Hixon, Margaret (2000). *Salote, Queen of Paradise*. University of Otago Press: Dunedin

Janman, Paul. (2012). *Tongan Ark*. Public Films.

Kaeppler, Adrienne (2014). *Sister Malia Tuifu'a: Descendant of Chiefs, Daughter of God*. Journal of the Polynesian Society Volume 123, Number 2

Latukefu, Rev. Dr. Sione. (1999). *Tonga at Independence and Now*. Moana, Volume 4, Spring 1999. University of Utah

Lomu, Jonah (2013). *Jonah My Story*. Hodder Moa Beckett: Auckland, NZ

Luomala, Katherine. (1955). *Voices on the Wind*. Bernice P. Bishop Museum: Honolulu, Hawaii

Mahina, 'Okusitino. (2004). *Reed Book of Tongan Proverbs*. Reed Publishing: Auckland.

Martin, John ed. (2012) *An Account of the Natives of the Tonga Islands* by William Mariner. Volume 2. Cambridge University Press: New York

Reed, A.W. (1974). *Myths and Legends of Polynesia*. A.H. & A.W.Reed: Wellington

Rutherford, Noel ed. (1977). *Friendly Islands: A History of Tonga*. Oxford University Press: Melbourne

Statham, Nigel ed. (2003). *A History of Tonga as Recorded by Rev John Thomas*.

Wood, Briar. (1998). *Heka He Va'a Mei Popo*. Women's Studies Journal 14 (2).

Wood-Ellem, Elizabeth ed. (2007). *Tonga and the Tongans: heritage and identity*. Tonga Research Association

My family: Lauano Sulufaleese Deborah, Maycee and Santana Riley. I love you guys so much!

Alby and Sue Riley, my parents, for giving me a strong foundation for life, and a love of reading.

Students and staff of Tangaroa College, Otara, Auckland, NZ.

Special thanks and 'ofa to Dr. Melenaite Taumoefolau, Dr. Adrienne Kaeppler and Dr.Judith Huntsman for your advice, assistance, guidance and support.

Michel Mulipola for the amazing illustrations and hooking up the meeting with Haku. It's been a blessing working with you again bro!

"Home Group" for spiritual encouragement: Ana and Rob Holloway and fanau; Ioka and Saulo Suamasi; and Iki, Moira and Sepora Valivaka.

To Joyce and Sinai Tonga: thanks for the advice about the cover and for giving Maycee and Santana a Tongan sister to hang out with!

Thank you to all who helped me with advice, encouragement, interviews, photos and stories and gave so freely of your time:

Emeline Afeaki-Mafile'o, Chris Anderson, Peter Brown, Shayne Bugden, PJ Chapman, Joseph Dawson, Alfred T. Day III, Dagmar Dyck, Valeria Edwards, Sione Faletau, Nanise Fifita, Ruha Fifita, Tonga Fifita, Mary Lyn Fonua, Shaun Higgins, David Hobby, Bill Hunter, Echo and Paul Janman, Karen Kay Management, Alison Kleczewski, Brian Langi, Hamish Macdonald, Karlo Mila, Kevin Moore, Tania McNamee, Jesoni Naga, Joe Naufahu, Matthew O'Sullivan, Fuli Pereira, Thibaut Plaire, Sue Reid, Hilary Scothorn, Rob Talkington, Ann Tarte, Filipe Tohi, John Tui, Manu Vatuvei, Ruben Wiki, Christopher and Kamelia Zarka.

Please forgive me if I have forgotten to mention someone.

And finally, much 'ofa to all the Tongan famili, friends, colleagues, teachers and students who have blessed me over the years, you know who you are, there's too many to name! You've played a part in the creation of this book.

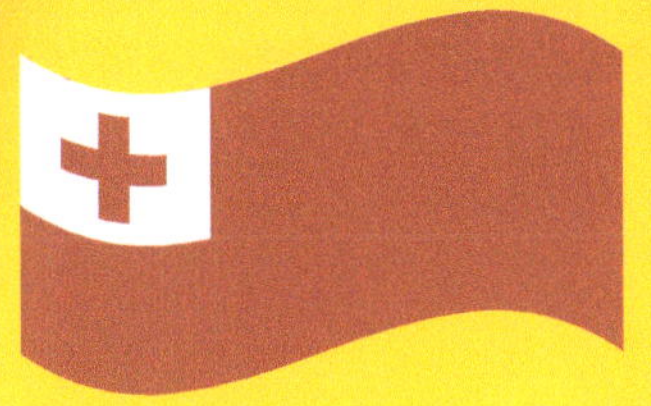

WRITER: DAVID RILEY

David grew up in Mangere, South Auckland. He has a Master of Arts in Social Anthropology from Auckland University where he focussed on Pacific culture and history. David has worked as a researcher for the MacMillan Brown Centre for Pacific Studies (Canterbury University) and as a freelance writer. He has 19 years' experience as a high school English and Drama teacher in South Auckland. In 2009, David's rap club for disengaged students featured on Television New Zealand. In 2011, his play, *Rock Bottom*, was shortlisted in Playmarket's Plays for the Young competition. In 2012, Little Island Press published David's first book for teenagers - *We Are the Rock,* a collection of profiles of achievers who have Niuean ancestry. In 2016, two of David's books – *Samoan Heroes* and *Jammin' with Steven Adams* - won Storylines Notable Book Awards. *Tongan Heroes* is his eleventh book to date.

ILLUSTRATOR: MICHEL MULIPOLA

Michel is a Samoan comic book artist based in Auckland, New Zealand. He won the 2006 Gibson Award for Best NZ Comic Book Artist and was a Grand Finalist in the 2013 Secret Walls x Aotearoa Live Art Battles.

He recently worked on an American graphic novel, Headlocked: The Last Territory.

When he isn't drawing, Michel can be found working at the Arkham City Comics store in Auckland and kicking butt as a pro wrestler for Impact Pro Wrestling New Zealand.

Check out his website at: www.bloodySamoan.com for more info.

IF YOU ENJOYED THIS BOOK, YOU MIGHT LIKE SOME OF MY OTHER WORK TOO!

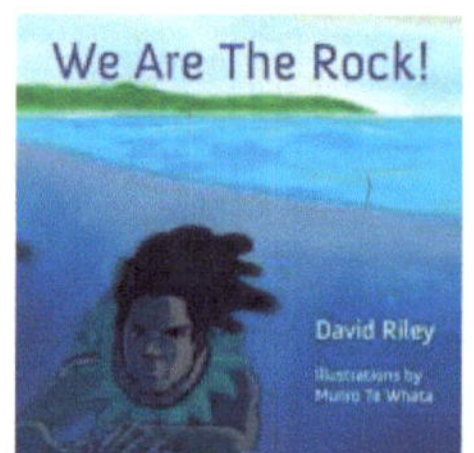
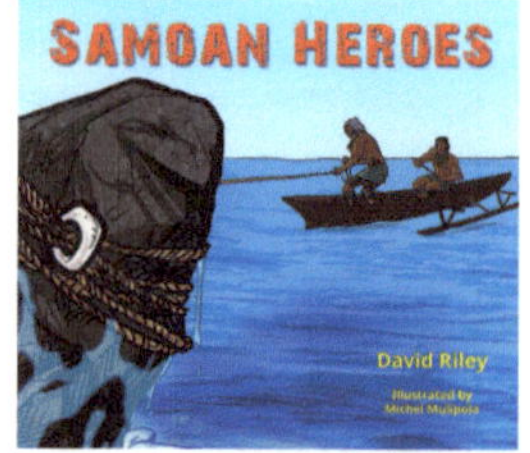

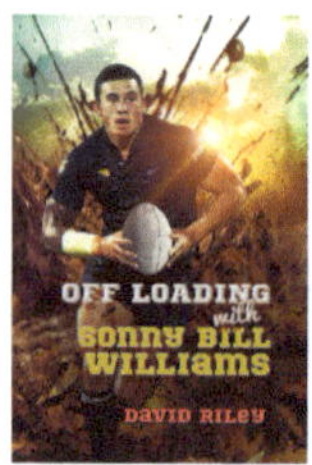
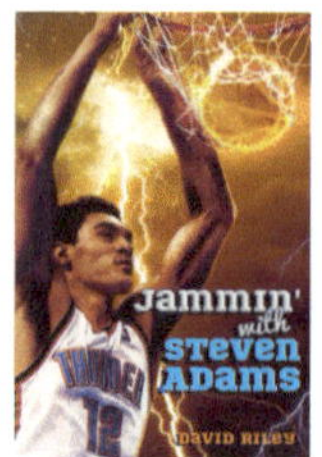

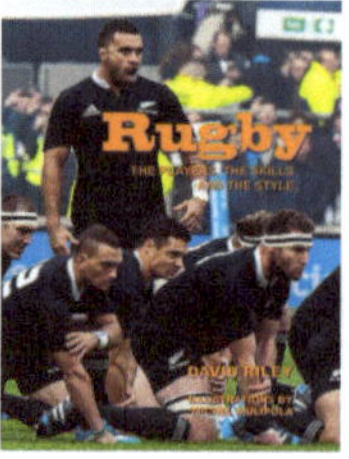
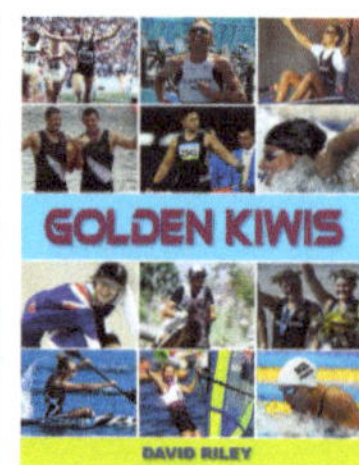

CONNECT WITH ME ONLINE:

Website: http://readingwarrior.com/

Twitter: https://twitter.com/DavidRileyNZ

Facebook: https://www.facebook.com/DavidRileyNZ

E mail: david@readingwarrior.com

Amazon Author page http://www.amazon.com/author/driley

READINGWARRIOR